# Theory
# and Practice

*By the Author*

THE STUDY OF COUNTERPOINT FROM FUX'S *Gradus ad Parnassum*
THE STUDY OF FUGUE

# Theory and Practice

## The Great Composer as Student and Teacher

# Alfred Mann

*Eastman School of Music*
*University of Rochester*

*W· W· Norton & Company · New York · London*

*Acknowledgments*

The facsimiles of Handel's music are reproduced with the permission of the Syndics of
the Fitzwilliam Museum, Cambridge, England.
The facsimiles of Beethoven's music and of Sechter's fugue dedicated to Schubert's memory are reproduced courtesy of the *Gesellschaft der Musikfreunde* in Vienna.

Published simultaneously in Canada by Penguin Books Canada Ltd, 2801 John Street, Markham, Ontario L3R IB4
Printed in the United States of America.

The text of this book is composed in Janson, with display type set in Modern #20.
Composition and manufacturing by The Maple-Vail Book Manufacturing Group.
Book design by B. Klein

First Edition

Library of Congress Cataloging-in-Publication Data

Mann, Alfred, 1917–
Theory and Practice.

Includes photoreprint of holography of Beethoven's
composition studies written under Haydn's direction.
1. Music—Theory—18th century—History and
criticism.   2. Music—Theory—19th century—
History and criticism.   3. Composition (Music)  4. Music—
18th century—History and criticism.   5. Music—19th
century—History and criticism.   I. Beethoven, Ludwig
van, 1770–1827.  Selections.  1987.  II. Title.
ML430.M28   1987     781      86–12584

ISBN 0-393-02352-4

W. W. Norton & Company, Inc., 500 Fifth Avenue, New York, N. Y. 10110
W. W. Norton & Company Ltd., 37 Great Russell Street, London WC1B 3NU

1 2 3 4 5 6 7 8 9 0

# Contents

# Foreword

*Look, gentlemen, that is the rule;*
*needless to say, I don't write that way.*

THIS remark by Anton Bruckner, as refreshingly direct as the broad Austrian dialect in which it was recorded by his student Heinrich Schenker, suggests a perplexing situation, and the personalities involved define the scene's protagonists: composer and theorist. Their roles had become mutually incompatible, and their disagreement familiar. The editors of *Tudor Church Music*, one of the principal collections of works by English Renaissance masters, prefaced their publication of liturgical music by Orlando Gibbons with an "admittedly carping introduction to the work of one who is universally reckoned among the greatest exponents of a great school;"[1] the reason was that the Elizabethan composer appeared to have violated certain principles of counterpoint. Artistic and didactic judgment had reached an impasse that proved impossible to resolve in the light of continuing advances in theory and practice.

My interest has long been directed to the situation that existed before the conflict arose. The suggestion to make it the subject of a book came from Paul Henry Lang who had witnessed the various preparatory studies required and given his generous help to many of them. We had met forty-five years ago, when I submitted to W. W. Norton a translation of the *Study of Counterpoint* from Johann Joseph Fux's *Gradus ad Parnassum*. There seemed to be a need for an English translation of the text; its fame was legendary, but it was not available to the modern student. The publisher was understandably skeptical about reissuing a work more than two hundred years old, but Lang's endorsement carried the day.

There was a growing awareness that eighteenth-century sources had been neglected, and renewed study of Fux's book led to an exploration of its impact upon the teaching of

[1] *Tudor Church Music*, P. C. Buck, E. H. Fellowes, A. Ramsbotham and S. Townsend Warner, eds. (London, 1925), IV, xxiv.

the classical composers. The discovery of major didactic documents from the hands of Handel, Mozart, and Schubert led me to the task of preparing critical editions of the manuscripts. The Beethoven anniversary in 1970 and the Bach anniversary in 1985, as well as the dramatic loss and restitution of Haydn manuscripts, prompted studies that helped round out a picture of the classical composer as student and teacher. Essential material for a conclusion to this book was provided by the opportunity to present unknown Tchaikovsky letters in *Music and Civilization: Essays in Honor of Paul Henry Lang*,[2] published on the occasion of the mentor's eightieth birthday.

The autograph of Beethoven's studies with Haydn, representing the extraordinary case in which both teacher and student are composers of supreme stature, forms the central portion of this study, and its discussion required a special manner of presentation. The document had not been previously published in its entirety, and for this reason its fifty-four pages are reproduced here in facsimile. The fact that it had not been treated kindly in standard works of Beethoven research and biography is, once again, due to the rivalry of theory and practice. The matter is rendered all the more complex by a curious mixture of common oversight and uncommon direction and execution: these are no ordinary lessons.

The nineteenth-century dilemma and its twentieth-century consequences have afforded the modern observer a detached view of the interrelationship of theory and practice, and it has become clear that today's acknowledged need to explore the history of performance practice is equal to the need for an investigation of didactic history.

I am indebted to many colleagues whose advice has guided me in the review and fresh use of earlier studies, and my special gratitude goes to W. W. Norton for genial support of my work from its inception to the issue of this volume. A word of thanks, finally, must go to the members of my Beethoven-Haydn seminar at the Eastman School of Music, and to Fontaine McNamara and Ruth Bleecker for help in preparing the manuscript for publication.

A.M.

---

[2] Edmond Strainchamps, Maria Rika Maniates and Christopher Hatch, eds. (New York, 1984).

# · I ·

# The Rise of
# Conventional Theory

DURING one of the opening scenes of *Faust*, Goethe merges the drama's principal characters: Mephistopheles poses as Faust. In a brief farce, the false teacher lectures a young student on theory and practice. Dismissing in turn logic, metaphysics, law, and theology, the conversation moves to medicine whose blunt advantages in meeting the fair sex are stressed by the master and readily grasped by the novice. Here the latter can see, as he says, the "wo und wie"—the "where and how," and Mephistopheles answers with the famous words, "Grau, teurer Freund, ist alle Theorie"—"Gray, my dear friend, is all theory."

A new attitude is caricatured in these lines, a criticism of theory that arose from the Age of Enlightenment. In an aside, the devil gives up "the dry tone" and with it the essence of his disguise—he turns from theory to practice. This attitude, so characteristic of the era, also began to play a major role in the teaching of musical composition. Commenting on his father's method of instruction, Carl Philipp Emanuel Bach wrote to the Bach biographer Johann Nicolaus Forkel on January 13, 1775:

> In composition he started his pupils right in with what was practical, and omitted all the *dry species* of counterpoint that are given in Fux and others.

Bach himself was reported to have used the same word, calling the fugues "of an old and hard-working contrapuntist *dry and wooden*."[1] But the fundamental distinction inherent in the son's remark is absent from the words of the father. Bach knew no theory of music, only practice, and the maligned species of counterpoint were presented in Johann Joseph Fux's celebrated *Gradus ad Parnassum* of 1725 as "musica activa"; the complementary term, "musica speculativa," was reserved by the author for the mathematical computations used to elucidate the nature of intervals.

[1] Friedrich Wilhelm Marpurg, in a letter to Johann Mattheson, *Kritische Briefe über die Tonkunst* (Berlin, 1760), I, 266. Translated in *The Bach Reader*, Hans T. David and Arthur Mendel, eds. (New York, 1966), p. 257.

1

"Speculation" is the equivalent of "theory." Derivatives from Latin and Greek, the two words designated the act of viewing, contemplating; and both "speculum" and "theoria" had served in earlier times as titles for musical treatises. Yet "music theory" in the sense that modern convention has given the term was not associated with instruction in the art of musical composition until the late eighteenth century; in fact, Mozart was not entirely conversant with this meaning of the term, whereas in Beethoven's studies it had gained importance.

What separated Bach and Handel from the masters of Viennese Classicism in their teaching of the craft was their exclusive commitment and individual orientation toward musical practice. Thus, C.P.E. Bach's judgment was based on a misconception. The four-part chorale harmonizations with which his father commenced the teaching of composition represented in fact a practice of musical performance conducted by the keyboard player, while the counterpoint species Fux devised for his students represented a purely vocal practice. Less well known than the *Gradus ad Parnassum* but closely related to its exercises is Fux's *Singfundament*, a collection of short motet studies, written without text and intended for the young musician in somewhat the same manner as Bach's Two-Part Inventions.

The concept of musical practice was in itself subjected to a radical division during the century preceding Bach and Handel. Attacked for his bold use of dissonance, Monteverdi declared his style of composition a "second practice" as opposed to the "first practice" of guarded dissonance treatment that marked the works of sixteenth-century composers. One might say that the two practices were eventually codified in the disciplines of harmony and counterpoint, but it took more than a century to arrive at precise didactic categories.

The seventeenth century witnessed a proliferation of musical styles, a widening of musical experience, that resulted from the rise of opera, accompanied solo song, and instrumental music. The first composer to be concerned not only with a clarification of styles but with their implications for the student of musical composition seems to have been Heinrich Schütz. In 1648, the aging composer published his *Geistliche Chormusik*, i.e. music in the old *a cappella* style, a series of motets to be performed, as he wrote, "without *bassum continuum*" (although by a stroke of curious irony his publisher, in the attempt to make the work more accessible, had a continuo part added in the printed score). As Schütz's preface indicated, the work was written with a decidedly pedagogical intent.

Continuo accompaniment had become the hallmark of the new style. Its use signalled the progressive tendencies of music drama, and an estrangement from firm contrapuntal control and the "requirements of a well-regulated composition," namely strict, free, and retrograde imitation, melodic inversion, invertible part-writing, and the simultaneous use of different themes. Schütz, who as a younger man had been one of the initiators of the "second" practice in the North, now found himself surrounded by a new generation of musicians well versed in the modern style. Unlike Schütz who had studied in Italy where the "first practice" remained a living tradition, the young practitioners of the art, working in a Germany physically and culturally exhausted by the Thirty Years War, lacked the "fundamenta" of their profession. Though it might seem like "heavenly harmony," music not founded in solid polyphonic technique was judged by Schütz to be no more than "an empty nutshell," and he admonished the beginner to "bite open that hard nut whose real substance is the foundation of good counterpoint."

His words represent a prophetic confrontation of the two terms. For a long time, "harmony" continued to be the word used to describe a fabric of independent part-writing. It was not until the publication of Jean Philippe Rameau's *Traité d'harmonie* in 1722 that the modern meaning was introduced. Three years later, Fux's *Gradus* established the modern didactic tradition of counterpoint. Yet this was also the decade in which Handel published his first set of harpsichord lessons, and in which Bach wrote the Inventions and the Clavier Books for his son Wilhelm Friedemann and his wife Anna Magdalena—the decade in which the last two great Baroque composers undertook a systematic exposition of instruction in composition. Though they both made their point of departure the highly-developed execution of figured bass, the technique remained, in their hands, inseparable from polyphonic practice. It did not serve to illustrate how voices are *placed* but how they *move* within a harmonic texture. And the balanced blending of harmony and counterpoint was to become the foremost challenge of conventional theory.

The new meaning of the word "theory" entered the study of music largely through the influence of a work which, despite its mixed reception, attained epochal significance: Johann Georg Sulzer's *General Theory of the Arts* (*Allgemeine Theorie der schönen Künste*, 1771–1774). The author, director of the Faculty of Philosophy at the Berlin Academy of Sciences, was guided by the ideals of Rousseau in his thesis that the arts must both express and enhance nature. In an approach typical of his time, he attempted to define all artistic terms and concepts that would serve this purpose and gathered them into an encyclopedic dictionary. His musical advisors, Johann Philipp Kirnberger and Kirnberger's student Johann Abraham Peter Schulz, represented a lineage of Bach's teaching. The system of musical theory they devised, however, came under immediate attack; it was questioned above all because Sulzer's basic axiom, namely that music is "a sequence of tones guided by the passions of sentiments," resisted his own scheme of standardization. In the second volume of an *Essay for the Instruction in Composition* (*Versuch einer Anleitung zur Composition*, 1782–1793), Heinrich Christoph Koch, one of the eminent writers of the period, formulated the critical argument:

The young composer's endeavors in letting his soul form beautiful melodies can never be truly aided by theory.

Nevertheless, music theory—no longer in the old sense of the "science" of music but as the subject of college and conservatory courses—became an established abstraction that was to dominate the teaching of musical composition in succeeding generations. This is all the more understandable since vital musical styles and techniques were changing swiftly to meet the demands of taste and musical imagination. When thoroughbass and fugue no longer represented current practice, they were relegated to the realm of theory. They were perpetuated in didactic thought much as the "stile antico" had been retained in the age of the second practice, but with a difference: the very terms "prima prattica" and "seconda prattica" implied that the old style had stayed alive, that it continued to be practicable and valid as an artistic expression. Counterpoint and fugue, as branches of modern theory, became "a metier, not an art."[2]

The dichotomy thus produced had more complex ramifications than this comparison might suggest. Beethoven, though he defied Johann Georg Albrechtsberger's teaching of fugue as an "art of creating musical skeletons,"[3] had been his attentive and dedicated student, and the Beethoven biographer Alexander Wheelock Thayer gives a description, authenticated by contemporary accounts, of Beethoven's daily sessions with a colleague and neighbor in which "the conversation usually turned upon musical theory and composition."[4]

Theory must here still be understood in rather general terms as the study of eighteenth-century writers on various subjects, not in the sense of a more-or-less fixed course of studies in different techniques. Mozart seems to have arrived at the conventional sequence of harmony and counterpoint in his pedagogical experience empirically—this sequence, though practiced at the time, had not been fully established. In teaching the young composer Thomas Attwood during the years 1785 and 1786, he became increasingly aware of a lack of linear skill in his student's harmonizations and—apparently under the influence of Haydn—decided to direct the twenty-one-year-old back to the beginning of contrapuntal studies.[5]

The most striking case of a composer's awareness of the increasing importance of conventional theory is Schubert's legendary lesson, two weeks before his death, with the respected Viennese theorist Simon Sechter. In a letter responding to a request for biographical information, Sechter mentioned this lesson but we had no knowledge of its contents until the manuscript pages on which both Schubert and Sechter had worked were recently brought to light.[6] Schubert turned to Sechter for advice because he was puzzled by certain technical details of fugal practice with which his generation was no longer conversant. The documentation of his lesson is all the more arresting since it shows that Schubert obtained the answers he sought. Sechter corrected the samples of fugal expositions that Schubert had submitted and added a clear exposition of the principles involved. The lesson was concluded with the assignment of a three-part fugue (see p. 148) on which Schubert was no longer able to work. It is a touching postlude to this remarkable encounter that Sechter carried out the assignment and published it, nine days after Schubert's death, in homage to the illustrious student—doubly touching because the mediocre quality of Sechter's work shows that teacher and student met merely as theorist and composer, but not on equal terms.

What had been revealed to the dying composer was a certain historical perspective

---

[2] Paul Henry Lang, *Music in Western Civilization* (New York, 1941), p. 974.
[3] Letter to the publishers B. Schott's Söhne, January, 1825.
[4] *Thayer's Life of Beethoven.* Rev. Elliot Forbes (Princeton, 1984), I, 262.
[5] Cf. This writer's discussion of Haydn's and Mozart's contrapuntal teaching in *Mozart-Jahrbuch* 1978 / 79, pp. 197 ff.
[6] The manuscript was discovered by the Schubert scholar Christa Landon; see her report "New Schubert Finds" in *Music Review* 31 (1970), pp. 215 ff.

that the rapid development of the classical style had temporarily obscured, and it was this historical perspective that gave to nineteenth-century theory its most valuable contributions. Albrechtsberger, Beethoven's teacher, had taken an important step in his teaching by adapting the modal technique of counterpoint to the modern tonalties of major and minor. This orientation was subsequently reversed by a historian, Heinrich Bellermann, who, in his manual *Der Contrapunkt* (1862), returned to the letter and spirit of Fux's *Gradus*. Bellermann, successor to Adolf Bernard Marx, the first professor of music at the University of Berlin and himself the author of a standard manual on composition, was followed in his restoration of modal counterpoint by several other writers, but his book was denounced as "obsolete at its very appearance" by his distinguished colleague Hugo Riemann—as obsolete, one might add, as Bach's conscious use of the modes in *Clavierübung III*.

In the end, neither historical nor analytical studies could solve the problems inherent in the ascendency of theory. It was the departure from practice that undermined the textbook literature of the nineteenth century. Composers of the Romantic age in their writings did not deal with the question of how to teach composition—only orchestration. Not until the twentieth century were teaching manuals again produced by prominent composers. That the element of creative thought had been missing in didactic literature is indicated in a treatise by Heinrich Schenker, foremost among twentieth-century theorists: *Neue musikalische Theorien und Fantasien* (1910–1920). Schenker, who had been torn in his early years between the careers of composer and theorist, eventually decided that the theorist's profession was for him a greater challenge. Though his work lives up to its title by offering a highly imaginative exposition of harmony and counterpoint, it inevitably points to the crux of the dilemma: in essence, composition must be taught by the composer; the theorist can only teach theory, no matter how refined the method.

Unlike theoretical guidance, practical guidance in the composer's craft is committed to the master-artisan relationship that was abandoned in textbook instruction. The didactic literature of earlier ages, too, was addressed to the individual, not to classes. The following chapters will thus be concerned with documents that show the time-honored direct and special exchange between teacher and student in an age when individualism, though strengthened in so many other ways, was abrogated in the teaching of musical composition.

# ·II·

# Bach and Handel

BACH and Handel were trained in the same tradition, but while there is some obvious similarity in their teaching material, their points of departure were quite different. With Bach, the emphasis is on the chorale; with Handel it is on suite and sonata movements. What is totally alike, however, is their attitude towards teaching. This is evident, on the one hand, from the fact that the study of composition was invariably linked to skill in active performance, and on the other hand, from the fact that both composers constantly rewrote their own works—as well as the works of others—with a view to changing performance requirements. The pervading practice of transcription, parody, and contrafactum—in short, rewriting—often meant rewriting with a correcting pen, and in this respect the composers treated their own works somewhat from the points of view of both teacher and student. The revision of details reveals in this era, more clearly than in any other, the practicing master of the craft, and even where Bach spotted a mistake in one of his works, his emendation is guided by an aesthetic premise rather than by a mere sense of "correction."

Nothing could illustrate this more clearly than a passage in the autograph of Bach's eight-part motet *Singet dem Herrn*, in which there is a double entry for a note in the highest voice (Example II–1). It is not easy to see that Bach actually crossed out the lower of the two notes. Thus, the editors of the old *Bach-Gesellschaft* edition were guided, like Bach himself, by the melodic pattern of the preceding measure and printed the note c. In the preparation of the text for the *Neue Bach-Ausgabe* it became clear that the former editors, again like Bach himself, had overlooked the parallel octaves in the dense double chorus texture and that the choice of the tone g and its more expressive turn of melody (and harmony) corresponded to the composer's wishes.

The change Bach made in this case is quite similar to one in which he mended parallel octaves in the work of a student. We have an invaluable example in a lesson in keyboard realization that Heinrich Nicolaus Gerber, father of the well-known music-lexicographer, carried out under Bach's supervision, for this is the only student manuscript in which entries from Bach's hand are preserved. The measures in question deal with the same problem (octaves between the bass and an upper part, or here rather, an inner part (Exam-

*Example II–1*

ple II–2). It is interesting that Bach's insistence on independent part-writing applies only to the keyboard accompaniment as such, and this reflects the continuo practice of his time: the keyboard player worked from a figured bass only, not from a score. Thus Bach's revisions are made without regard for the melodic line of the obbligato part in the top line,

*Example II–2*

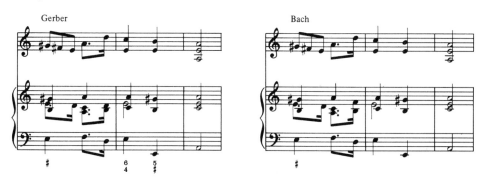

*Example II–3*

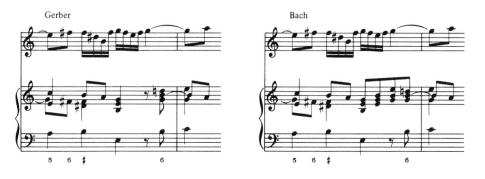

*Example II–4*

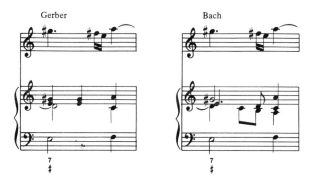

but the integrity and enrichment of the keyboard part is his ever-present concern (Examples II–3 and II–4).

Bach's revisions in Gerber's manuscript parallel variants in a vast number of works from his hand, and our consequent awareness of his general working procedure offers ample compensation for the scant documentation we have from actual lessons. Particularly close to Bach's direct instruction are some examples of chorale harmonization in which Bach did not write a new setting but rewrote an existing one. Recent investigations have shown that Bach used on several occasions a Leipzig hymnal compiled in 1682 by Gottfried Vopelius, cantor at St. Nicolai, adopting not only melodies but also harmonizations for chorales in his cantatas.[1] In some cases, Bach's score remains entirely faithful to the original; in others, the model becomes a veritable student's manuscript transformed by editorial touches that overwhelmingly demonstrate the presence of the master (Examples II–5 and II–6).

The design of Bach's teaching is recorded in considerable detail by students and copyists. C.P.E. Bach wrote in his letter of January 13, 1775, to Johann Nicolaus Forkel:

---

[1] See Emil Platen, "Zur Echtheit einiger Choralsätze Johann Sebastian Bachs," *Bach-Jahrbuch* 1975, pp. 50 ff.

*Example II–5*

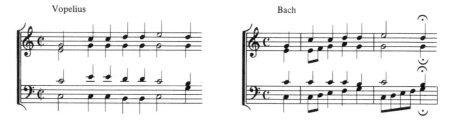

*Example II–6*

His pupils had to begin their studies by learning pure four-part thoroughbass. From this he went to chorales; first he added the basses to them himself, and they had to invent the alto and tenor. Then he taught them to devise the basses themselves.

In his own account, Forkel, again on the basis of communications from Bach's sons, goes into specific points of technique:

Under certain circumstances he could not even endure covered octaves and fifths between the middle parts, which, otherwise, we at the most attempt to avoid between the two extreme parts; under other circumstances, however, he wrote them down so plainly that they offended every beginner in composition, but afterwards soon justified themselves.

Bach introduced his students to the basic principles of part-writing through a compendium which has been preserved in two copies. The earlier one was written down by Anna Magdalena Bach (and completed by a copyist). Entitled "Some Most Necessary Rules of Thorough Bass by J. S. B.," it systematically lists the common combinations of figures used for thoroughbass harmonization, how they may be expanded, and what doublings to avoid. The later and larger one is a manuscript once owned by Johann Peter Kellner whose copies of various Bach works constitute important sources. It contains, in an unidentified hand, a number of exercises which, as is evident from their poor execution, were not reviewed by Bach.[2] What is readily discernible from the Kellner manuscript, however, is that Bach stressed a richness of thoroughbass texture, unusual for his period, but well known to us from his own works.

[2] Both manuscripts were published in Philipp Spitta, *Johann Sebastian Bach*, trans. Clara Bell and J. A. Fuller-Maitland (1873–80), reprint (New York, 1951), II, 315 ff.

Demonstrating the characteristically full sound of Bach's keyboard realizations, the manuscript contains exercises based on complete bass scales to be harmonized tone by tone (in the thoroughbass practice of the time known as the "Rule of the Octave") in which even sequences of sixth-chords, normally realized only in three parts, are given as examples for *Enquatre Playing* (i.e., four-part realization). To the examples, which contain only the bass line, specific instructions are added, such as:

For the first set marked with 6, the sixth may be doubled, but for every alternate group the octave is to be taken, and continued to the end.

*Example II–7*

For a rising octave scale with alternating sixths and fifths, the instruction reads:

The player must begin quite high up with the right hand, and proceed *per motum contrarium;* the octave is to be taken with the sixth.

*Example II–8*

The unreliability of the source is undoubtedly reflected in the following comment by a modern interpreter:

This would be sheer nonsense were the figuring of the example correct . . . what Bach beyond any possibility of doubt intended was as follows:[3]

*Example II–9*

[3] F. T. Arnold, *The Art of Accompaniment from a Thorough-Bass* (London, 1931), p. 584.

Yet this comment is mistaken. We are obviously concerned, in this phase of the studies, with consonant chord combinations only, and the lack of reliability is likely not so much in the copying of basses or figures but in the realizations of basses presented. Again, exemplifying Bach's demanding style of keyboard realization, the manuscript includes thoroughbass assignments to be carried out in a fugal manner. We also encounter this type of assignment in Handel's composition lessons. But the nature of the completed assignments, recorded in the Kellner manuscript as having emanated from Bach's instruction, makes it clear that Bach did not see the student's work.

"Oh, Bach, Sebastian Bach, dear lady!," cried Edmund Pfühl, organist at St. Mary's, as he strode up and down the salon with great activity . . . "Certainly, as you say, it was he through whom the victory was achieved by harmony over counterpoint. He invented modern harmony, assuredly. But how? Need I tell you how? By progressive development of the contrapuntal style—you know it as well as I do. Harmony? Ah, no! By no means. Counterpoint, my dear lady, counterpoint!"

This passage from Thomas Mann's famous novel *Buddenbrooks* offers a vignette of Romantic controversy in defining Bach's style. But in the words of Pfühl, an imaginary successor to Buxtehude at St. Mary's in Lübeck who serves as music master to the young Hanno Buddenbrook, the critical terms are still confused, and it is amusing to consider that the concept of independent part-writing that in his monologue emerges victorious was, as we have mentioned, designated as harmony in Bach's usage. "Contrapunctus" was a term Bach employed only occasionally; he reserved it for sections of the *Art of Fugue*, as he had chosen "Ricercare" for similar sections in the *Musical Offering*. Bach's use of these terms marks the conservative tendencies of the retrospective artist, respected but isolated, that is recaptured in the figure of Pfühl. "The little book on the church modes he had written and given into print, was recommended for private study at two or three conservatories," and in the course of the story he grudgingly appends to it, after some outbursts about the "insanity" of Tristan, a chapter "on the application of the old modes to Richard Wagner's church- and folk-music"—an outcome of his arguments with Frau Buddenbrook, an ardent Wagnerian.

More interesting than the musical is the social aspect of these scenes: the resistance of Konsul Buddenbrook against his wife's and son's alliance with Pfühl is not unlike the stand Handel's father took against his son's wishes to devote his life to music. Handel's early biographer, John Mainwaring, reports that it took considerable urging from the Duke of Saxe-Weissenfels, whom Handel's father served as court physician, to have the young Handel apprenticed to Friedrich Wilhelm Zachau at St. Mary's in Halle. Yet there is a critical difference in the status of the Halle St. Mary organist and the Lübeck St. Mary organist in the novel: Zachau did not appear at the salon in Handel's home once or twice a week, as Pfühl appears in the Breite Strasse, but the student went to the church, probably every day. That the practice of such intense training had begun to decline is implied in the words of Hanno's mother upon engaging the teacher: "I know there are two or three people here in town who give lessons—women, I think. But they are simply piano teachers."

It was the bourgeois milieu of music lessons that Handel himself faced in later years at Hamburg, Lübeck's sister city in the Hanseatic league. Not being attached to either church or court service, as was customary for a composer of Handel's time, Handel may have looked upon his students like the hero of a later novel who divided the artistic clientele into "Klaviergänse," "Singgänse," and "Malgänse"—piano-playing geese, singing geese, and painting geese.[4] At least, this is suggested in his remark to a colleague who had studied with Georg Philipp Telemann and Johann Mattheson in Hamburg:

After I had left your hometown anno 1709 in order to go to Italy and eventually enter service at the court of Hanover, no power on earth could have moved me to take up teaching duties again—except Anne, the flower of all princesses.[5]

Mainwaring speaks of Handel's "noble spirit of independency." He was independent indeed, and he had turned down the offer of a Tuscan prince to travel with him from Hamburg to Italy, indicating that he would go "as soon as he could make a purse for that occasion." He paid for his independence in part by giving the lessons he so heartily disliked, and there is some irony in the fact that what caused his conversion in matters of pedagogy was his appointment as Royal Music Master to the British court.

Princess Anne, eldest daughter of George II and a cousin of Frederick the Great, became Handel's student, probably at the age of eleven. She remained the composer's friend throughout her life, and her unusual gift and personality prompted Handel to write out a set of manuscripts, carefully preserved, in which the rudiments of the art of composition are presented with extraordinary precision and beauty of penmanship.

Thus the documentation of Handel's teaching offers a picture that is the exact opposite of that of Bach's teaching. Studies published a generation ago have identified more than eighty personal pupils of Bach's; a number of them became recognized composers and teachers in their own right. Through their writings and study books, the master's instruction was perpetuated, but only a handful of examples bearing Bach's autograph annotations exist. Handel had very few students of a professional calibre, and only one of them, John Christopher Smith, transmitted his teacher's instruction. The exercises he copied are taken directly from Handel's autograph, and while their compilation may have originated in the course of Smith's own training under Handel, they were apparently subjected to considerable refinement in the lessons for Princess Anne. The studies presented below (pp. 21 ff) have been preserved in several versions from Handel's hand as well as in faithful copies made by Smith when he, in turn, assumed the post of Royal Music Master.[6]

[4] Florian Mayr, in Ernst von Wolzogen's Liszt novel, *Der Kraft-Mayr* (Stuttgart, 1927), p. 31.
[5] Jacob Wilhelm Lustig, *Inleiding tot de Muziekkunde* (Groningen, 1771), p. 172. Cf. Friedrich Chrysander, *G. F. Händel* (Leipzig, 1858–67), II, 364. 1709 was apparently a date incorrectly remembered; it should read 1706.
[6] The complete set of Handel autographs was published in the *Hallische Händel-Ausgabe;* copies made by Smith were reproduced in "Handel's Successor: Notes on John Christopher Smith the Younger," in *Music in Eighteenth-Century England,* C. Hogwood and R. Luckett, eds. (Cambridge, 1982).

Handel's collection of assignments in thoroughbass and fugue is neatly divided into groups, so that a sequence of technical phenomena emerges with clarity. The basic phenomenon is what in Handel's time was called the "harmonic triad": the triad in root position. As the concept of inversion is applied to the triad, it becomes evident that in Handel's view only one of the triad tones qualifies for the procedure, namely the third; inversion of the octave would produce merely a duplication of the same tone, while inversion of the fifth results in the fourth, which Handel treats essentially as a dissonance.

Dissonance, however, is not dealt with as an isolated problem of thoroughbass realization (there is no specific discussion of dissonant chords) but as an integral part of all study phases. Passing and neighboring dissonances are introduced with the opening presentation of the triad in root position, and the suspended chord enters the course and studies with the same ease as the altered chord. Chromaticism and suspension through seventh-chord inversions appear simply as attributes of fluent part-writing, and the interval of the seventh itself is not introduced with the connotation of constituting a new "chord" but as a suspension of the sixth, just as the fourth is introduced as a suspension of the third (Examples II–10, II–11, II–12, and II–13).

*Example II–10*

(Thoroughbass Lessons, No. *1*)

*Example II–11*

(No. *9*)

*Example II–12*

(No. *14*)

*Example II–13*

(No. *15*)

Consequently, even the technique of part-writing in imitation is naturally, but quite clearly, suggested in the thoroughbass exercises (Examples II–14, II–15, and II–16). They

*Example II–14*

(No. *12*)

*Example II–15*

(No. *15*)

*Example II–16*

(No. *23*)

are concluded with three larger assignments which give the impression of complete suite or sonata movements, and only these could to some extent be considered a study of chords such as $^6_4$, $^7_3$, and $^4_2$ (Examples II–17, II–18, and II–19), but even here the appearance of passing dissonance is maintained in each case. Thoroughbass, in Bach's and Handel's practice, remains a study in part-writing, and it leads directly to the study of fugue.

How direct a connection exists between Handel's thoroughbass and fugue exercises is stressed by the fact that the sequence of 7-6 suspensions that formed one of the thoroughbass assignments (No. *15*) is recast as a fugal exposition in the first fugue assignment. The

*Example II–17*

(No. *22*)

*Example II–18*

(No. *23*)

*Example II–19*

(No. *24*)

course of studies is so tightly constructed that Handel repeatedly derives new examples from those given in preceding sections. In this case he completes the opening measures himself up to the point of the last entrance, which is saved for the bass, in order to continue the example in a manner identical to portions of the earlier exercise, but with the obvious implication that the bass realization is to represent a fugal fabric. In subsequent assignments, he outlines the exposition by marking the voices in capital letters, C (*Cantus*, i.e. Soprano), A, T, B, and by fixing their entrance tones through the symbols of German organ tablature in adding above the respective letters, as needed, one or two short lines (the first or second octave above middle c; small letters without lines serve for the octave below middle c, capital letters for the octave below that)—a practice that reflects his own training under Zachau. That this method also includes more subtle directions is shown in the second assignment (p. 28) in which the sequence of given entrances includes the procedure of tonal answer.

In the third fugal exercise (p. 28), the tonal design is further emphasized through the assignment of two complete expositions, and the eventual return to the tonic is accentuated by a reverse order of the melodic forms of theme and answer—in the fugal practice of the time known as the inversion of fugal answers. At this point in the studies, Handel supplied the student with fully executed examples to illustrate particular problems of structure.

The larger form involving two expositions requires an overall design in which renewed entrances of parts receive added clarity through rests. The principle of such systematic interruptions within the fugal texture is shown in an example, written in the same key, whose structure corresponds to that of the assignment and from whose theme, in turn, that of the following assignment (No. *4*) is derived.

The fugal assignments end with two exercises in double fugue which exemplify two patterns of thematic dualism: the two themes are distinguished by their rhythmic and melodic conformation (No. *5*), or—in a more complex constellation—they are contrasted in rhythm only, whereas the melodic shape of the countersubject is plainly drawn from the theme itself (No. *6*). In both cases, the assignment is again accompanied by Handel's illustration. The latter one is developed from a series of sketches in which the melodic outline of the theme seems to have been achieved by trial and error. The first few measures of a short setting, which he drafted as an example for the imitation and augmentation of a theme, show a number of changes entered in the process of composition (Example II–20).

What apparently happened was that Handel realized that the close imitation of the original melodic sequence would lead to a dissonant fourth in the second measure (Example II–21) and that even the change of melody on which he then decided would produce dissonances with the imitating voice (Example II–22). Thus he spaced the entrances more widely and wrote a four-part exposition that leads with miraculous ease to augmentation of the melodic component contained in the second measure (by melodic inversion) in alto and bass, and to double augmentation in soprano and tenor (Example II–23). In applying the theme to the texture of double fugue, he first wrote out a brief fragment using a sharply

*Example II–20*

*Example II–21*                                              *Example II–22*

*Example II–23*

*Example II–24*

contrasting countersubject (Example II–24) and, subsequently, the example given in No. 6 whose themes are directly linked throughout by alternating diminution and augmentation.

As a final example, Handel added the first draft for one of his own published works. It is a fugue which he composed in open score notation (as did Bach in various examples preserved in that form) and which breaks off after thirty-eight measures—a conclusion is hastily sketched in a four-measure fragment suggesting pedal point and cadence (see p. 36). This offers the most interesting detail of the piece: in the printed version, Handel used the motif at the end of the bass part as a second subject, thus transforming the fugue written on a single theme into a double fugue. Mattheson, not aware that the draft for the fugue on a single theme existed, praised the printed version as setting a model for double fugue composition:

Who would imagine that these few notes contain a compact braid of gold, a thread that may be spun out to reach a hundred times its length?[7]

---

[7] *Der Vollkommene Capellmeister* (Hamburg, 1739), p. 440.

This is not the only instance when an original work by Handel appeared in the examples he used for teaching. The thoroughbass exercise no. *22* is reminiscent of a slow movement from the *Concerto Grosso* op. 6, no. 11, and the fugue assignment no. *6* brings to mind an aria from *Riccardo Primo* as well as choruses from *Messiah, Samson,* and the *Foundlings Hospital Anthem.* Two of the trio sonatas ascribed to Bach are written upon a bass from one of Bach's violin sonatas, and the trio versions may in fact represent figured-bass studies upon a "cantus firmus" that the composer had assigned to various students. Such a procedure is all the more plausible since Bach's pupils worked regularly with chorale melodies which the master had used himself. But the direct use of materials from the composer's workshop begins to fade by the middle of the century. Bach's thoroughbass instruction refers to a "Musical Manual" *(Musikalische Handleitung)* published by one of his contemporaries, Friedrich Erhard Niedt, in 1700. With Haydn's and Mozart's didactic work, the emphasis shifts more decidedly to the use of printed literature, and above all to Fux's *Gradus ad Parnassum* which, though itself still tied to the practice of performance, paved the way for the ascendance of theory in the teaching and study of the composer.

# Handel's Lessons for Princess Anne
# Thoroughbass and Fugue

## *Thoroughbass*

### *Triads in Root Position*

### *Alteration of Triads*

*Inversion of the Third*

*Suspension of the Third*

*Suspension of the Inverted Third*

*Suspension Chains and Octave Suspension*

*Pedal Point*

# Fugue

*1: Assignment*

*2. Assignment*

*3: Assignment*

*3: Example*

4: *Assignment*

5: *Assignment*

5: *Example*

6: *Assignment*

*6: Example*

*Fugue from Handel's Keyboard Suite No. II:*
*Manuscript Draft*

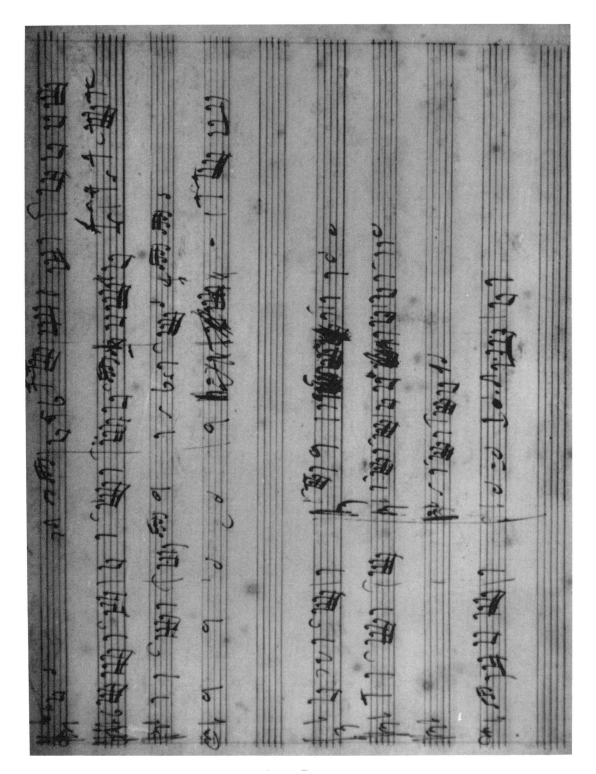

*Fugue from Handel's Keyboard Suite No. II:*
*Published Version (1720)*

# · III ·

# Haydn and Mozart

HAYDN's teaching assumed a key role in the didactic trends of the eighteenth century. Johann Joseph Fux was still living when Haydn began his training as a choirboy at St. Stephan's in Vienna. Fux had held office at the Cathedral for more than thirty years, and his influence was ever present. Haydn was instructed from the pages of Fux's *Singfundament;* he heard Fux's Masses, and upon gaining some independence as a young student, he obtained a copy of Fux's *Gradus ad Parnassum* which he studied intensely.

In his *Biographische Notizen über Joseph Haydn*, taken down from conversations with the composer and published a year after Haydn's death, Georg August Griesinger relates how the young Haydn in his attic room "envied no king his lot," and he speaks of the "tireless exertion" with which Haydn went through the pages of Fux's *Gradus:*

He worked his way through the whole method, did the exercises, put them by for several weeks, then looked them over again and polished them until he thought he had got them right.[1]

In the process, Haydn entered a wealth of annotations in the book, and he must have added to them throughout his life because some comments refer to his early training under the Viennese chapelmaster Georg Reutter and others to Kirnberger's writings which were not published until Haydn was in his fifties. These marginalia have been preserved only through copies since Haydn's "well-worn volume" was destroyed by flames in the Second World War. But in preparation of his Haydn biography, Carl Ferdinand Pohl had faithfully reproduced them in another copy of the work which is now in the archival collection of the *Gesellschaft der Musikfreunde* in Vienna. A second manuscript reproduction was recently discovered in the *Gradus* copy owned by the library of Smith College, Northampton, Massachusetts. In its style of handwriting, it suggests an earlier date of origin than Pohl's entries; it might well have been made during Haydn's lifetime, and its details are more precise than those related by Pohl: there are portions in which the Haydn biographer

[1] *Joseph Haydn: Eighteenth-Century Gentleman and Genius.* A translation by Vernon Gotwals of *Biographische Notizen über Joseph Haydn* by G. A. Griesinger and *Biographische Nachrichten von Joseph Haydn* by A. C. Dies (Madison, 1963), p. 10.

apparently could not decipher the composer's writing and where he found himself compelled to trace the graphic outline of the remarks without understanding their content, whereas in the Smith College copy they are intelligibly rendered.

The existence of this copy suggests that Haydn's own volume was lent out on occasion for purposes of study—as shall be discussed below, it is likely that for a time it passed into the hands of Mozart. The document in its copied form offers such a remarkable contrast to the volumes owned by Padre Martini, Mozart's teacher, and Leopold Mozart that we are patently dealing with totally different situations. In the latter cases, the work remained a "library book" which was not regularly drawn into the practical teaching situation or subjected to intense use. With Haydn, the opposite applies; in addition to his scrupulous commentary, Haydn prepared an abstract of portions from the text, to which we will return in the discussion of Beethoven's studies. Thus the composer who was born before the youngest Bach son and who died in the year that saw the publications of Beethoven's Fourth, Fifth, and Sixth Symphonies, was the mentor through whom the didactic heritage of the Baroque passed directly to later generations. Among his numerous students were the brothers of Carl Maria von Weber.

Haydn's commentary on Fux's *Gradus* contains two basic types of entry. One, probably written largely in Haydn's younger years, deals with correction and explanation of the verbal and musical text itself, and in these notations we witness the extraordinary thoroughness with which Haydn examined the work. Fux explains in his preface that he had prevailed on the diligence of friends for proofreading. But the painstaking amendments contained in the printed and rather extensive *Errata* listing are far surpassed by Haydn's minute emendations. Haydn corrects mistakes that had crept even into the *Errata* listing, and he spots errors that had escaped Fux's attention in music examples he had quoted from his own works.

The other type of entry suggests that in later periods, Haydn studied the work again from a critical point of view that shows the experienced composer rather than the student. Yet the two attitudes merge: it is invariably Haydn's conscientious checking that leads to questions in which his creative judgement comes into play. A false use of the cambiata resolution, for instance, calls to Haydn's attention a context in which Fux intended to use this figure for motivic imitation (Example III–1). The same sense of consistency leads Haydn to restore the melodic line of a fugal theme (Example III–2). That the note f is in fact a printer's error in this case is confirmed by the anticipation of the note d as the typical "guide" placed at the end of the preceding line—the mistake occurred at the beginning of a new line and had remained uncorrected.

*Example III–1*

*Example III–2*

But there is more involved than the correction of one note. The erroneous passage runs counter to an important principle of fugal design (illustrated, for instance, in Handel's fugal studies, p. 28 f.), a principle which in Fux's own text is discussed in detail:

. . . it is necessary after a rest to introduce either the old subject or some new subject, which must then be taken up also by the other parts, if you do not want to make yourself open to the reproving words of the gospel of St. Matthew (22:12): "Friend, how camest thou in hither not having a wedding garment?"

The argument goes back to sources as early as Thomas Morley's *A Plain and Easy Introduction to Practical Music* (1597) where we find its first detailed explanation:

. . . the odd rest giveth an unspeakable grace to the point . . .[2]

---

[2] Thomas Morley, *A Plain & Easy Introduction to Practical Music*, ed. Alec Harman (New York, 1973), p. 161.

"Point" in Morley's terminology stands for "fugal theme," and he formulates the reason for what became a rule applied to fugal structure:

. . . it is supposed that when a man keepeth long silence and then beginneth to speak he will speak to the purpose . . .[3]

It is this rule with which Haydn was concerned, both in this case and in the first of two fugues from the *Gradus ad Parnassum*. These two fugues must have offered special points of interest to Haydn, and here we are not concerned with mistake and correction but with the true essence of the study situation: a dialogue between two composers. The nature of fugal statement and answer poses difficulties in the first fugue at the passage on which Haydn comments. An entrance on the note a in the second part of the measure is precluded by the six-four chord in which it would result. Nor is an entrance on the tone b possible—aside from constituting an unprepared dissonance, it would alter the established balance of theme and answer. Fux resorts to the device of an irregular entrance using both tones in succession. Thus he does achieve the proper beginning of the statement on a, though finding himself unable to sustain the tone, he fills in the interval of the third with which this statement would normally begin and introduces the tone b as a passing dissonance (Example III–3).

The procedure is entirely in keeping with Baroque practice (we find it, for instance in the answer for the fugal theme in Bach's *Chromatic Fantasy and Fugue*). That Haydn takes exception to it, marking the entrance "Licentia non bona" shows the clashing of two stylistic orientations. The composer of the Baroque saw nothing wrong in letting the *cantabile* ideal or harmonic considerations take precedence over strictness of imitation. In fact, harmonic logic had triumphed over melodic logic in establishing the Baroque practice of tonal answer. The latter, however, had begun to turn into a typical concept of theory for the composers of the Viennese Classical period: though sanctioned by the needs of the tonal language, a deviation from the strict form of the fugal theme required rules; a casual deviation remained a "license."

Whereas Haydn differs with Fux in this instance, he reinforces Fux's thinking in the second fugue. Fux's examples illustrate the principle of gradually tightening sequences of

*Example III–3*

Lic: non bona

(see p. 53)

[3] *Ibid*.

fugal entrances. He favors a design of three expositions in which the second shows a closer succession of theme and answer than the first and in which the third exposition is formed by stretto imitation. In the second exposition of the fugue in C, Haydn discovered the possibility of a thematic entrance that Fux had overlooked, and he carries out what Fux seemed to have intended: with the change of a single note, he completes a second exposition and strengthens the structure of the entire example (Example III–4).

*Example III–4*

(Haydn)

etc.

etc.

(see p. 54)

Haydn's annotations in Fux's fugues bear a semblence to those that Mozart entered in three fugal examples written by his student Thomas Attwood. In the first of these, Mozart, like Haydn, supplied a single note to restore a thematic entrance (Example III–5.) In the

*Example III–5*

(see p. 57)

second, his correction is at first concerned with the opposite: the thematic entrance results in such awkward part-writing that Mozart gives preference to a "license," though he makes a change two measures later in order to maintain a developing eighth-note-figure imitation (Example III–6). In the third fugue Mozart made similar emendations; he corrected the poor part-writing, but while his second entry begins with a correction of parallel octaves, he goes on to strengthen the entire texture, using a stretto reference to the chromatic theme (Examples III–7a and III–7b).

*Example III–6*

(see p. 58)

*Example III–7a*

(Mozart)

*etc.*

*etc.*

*etc.*

(see p. 59)

*Example III–7b*

(Mozart)

(see p. 60)

Neither Haydn nor Mozart, however, seem to have dealt with fugue as a systematic teaching discipline. Both of them had wrestled with the genre in their early quartets, and they must have considered the problem of fugal form the province of the experienced composer, not the novice. Samuel Wesley, Attwood's contemporary and London colleague, has left an interesting testimony, preserved in a British Library manuscript:

Mr. Thomas Atwood, his Majesty's Organist, who studied in Germany under Mozart, related to me many years ago an anecdote of his which frequently recurs to memory. Being naturally anxious to make a rapid progress under such a master and such a genius, he soon observed to Mozart, "Sir, I am extremely desirous to produce a good fugue from your instructions"—to which he replied, "Do not be too much in a hurry—study plain counterpoint for about twelve months, and then it will be quite time enough to talk about fugues."[4]

Mozart evidently adopted many of Haydn's didactic principles. The close association of the two Viennese masters began in the 1780s when both of them had taken up permanent residence in Vienna. It was at this time that Mozart began a concentrated exploration of Fux's text. The study book which an earlier pupil compiled under Mozart's guidance in 1784 contains only a brief reference to examples from the *Gradus*, but the Attwood studies demonstrate the full extent of Fux's course in contrapuntal training and a striking affinity to Haydn's marginalia. Of particular interest is the similarity in certain details that form elaborations upon Fux's text and, in some cases, deviations from it. Even the same modification of one of Fux's *cantus firmi* has come down from Haydn's and Mozart's hands, and we are led to the conclusion that in the course of discussions about didactic matters, Mozart examined Haydn's annotated *Gradus* copy with the greatest care.

  For actual teaching purposes Haydn had extracted from Fux's book only the section dealing with counterpoint, and Mozart's practical use of the *Gradus* material likewise ends with the completion of exercises in four-part counterpoint. The fugal examples from the Attwood studies mentioned above exhibit a totally different provenance. On a stipend

[4]"Thomas Attwoods Theorie-und Kompositionsstudien bei Mozart," *Neue Mozart-Ausgabe* (Kassel, 1969), Kritischer Berischt, p. 48.

granted by the Prince of Wales, the gifted young organist had journeyed to Italy and studied for two years with two Neapolitan composers, Filippo Cinque and Gaetano Lattila. Evidently dissatisfied with the results, he had gone for further study to Vienna where he began lessons with Mozart in 1786. Possibly in order to show the level of competence he had achieved, he presented to Mozart several fugues that he had written in the course of his instruction under Latilla. In Mozart's comments, we become aware of a schism in teaching traditions that arose in the eighteenth century. The dialogue of Fux's *Gradus* contains one particular exchange between student and teacher which, in its brevity, characterizes the situation:

"I have often heard that the study of fugue is not familiar to all professors of the art of music."

"That is true. Oratory on this subject is more common than knowledge."

Fux's amused irony is aimed at the Italian *professori* and at the decline of contrapuntal teaching in the south. The tradition emanating from the Italian Renaissance masters, and with it the perfection of fugal art, had moved to the north, and so it was in northern countries that the modern pedagogy of fugal writing developed. In Italy, the "stile antico" had remained, as we have said, alive, and what the student of fugue used as models were the conservatively-oriented motets and Masses of the Catholic service, not examples from the great organ literature.

Padre Martini's famous *Esemplare o sia saggio fondamentale prattico di contrappunto*, a "Fundamental Practical Essay on Counterpoint," was published in two volumes. The first, issued in 1774, deals with counterpoint upon a *cantus firmus*; the second, issued in 1775, with fugal counterpoint. In contrast to the German didactic practice of the time, counterpoint and fugue were in fact not separated; both were designated "counterpoint." Their presentation as two distinct disciplines is further qualified by the fact that there are no exercises or assignments: all examples are quoted from existing literature. The first volume is concerned with works which contain Gregorian chant, and the second with works that do not. While the latter offer instructive illustrations of fugal procedure at various points, they are not "fugues" according to the later commonly accepted norm—they usually begin with a full setting involving all voices—and the matter of fugal form or design is not discussed.

In the hands of lesser figures, this method was apt to lead to a certain deterioration of technique, whereas Martini's own teaching maintained an exemplary level, as is evident in his instruction of Johann Christian Bach and especially in his encounter with the young Mozart. For the fourteen-year-old this encounter opened a new world, and the studies that followed were of lasting influence upon his creative career.

It was under Martini's guidance that Mozart was invited to become a member of the famed *Accademia dei Filarmonici* which had been founded a hundred years earlier, and his test piece for admission constitutes one of the most remarkable documents in the history of contrapuntal studies. A four-part antiphon composition in which *cantus firmus* and fugal setting were to merge had to be written in traditional style within a limited time while the candidate was locked in a room with no recourse to an instrument. It has been suggested that Mozart's solution was actually written by Martini, but the strict circumstances of the examination made such an act patently impossible. Martini's help was of a different kind: in what amounted to an ideal counterpoint lesson, he rewrote the finished work, and both Mozart's and Martini's versions have been preserved.

The comparison bears witness to both the unusual gift of the student and the unusual experience and pedagogical insight of the teacher. The most immediately apparent difference is the brevity of Mozart's initial elaboration of the theme. In the third measure he takes up a new one which, in turn, finds no room for elaboration; it recurs sporadically, but remains—due to its instrumentally-conceived melody which runs into hidden fifths and octaves with the other voices—a somewhat foreign element in the composition (Example III–8). Martini's second subject grows from the augmentation of the first (Example III–9). Thus it provides not only thematic by stylistic unity, a fact which is underlined by his avoidance of chromaticism and other accentuated means that Mozart uses, such as the Neapolitan sixth. The work attained balance of melody, harmony, and structural planning.

The influence of contrapuntal studies upon Mozart's work can be seen in three distinct phases: the first impetus, resulting from the meetings with Martini; the association with Haydn, beginning in the early 1780s; and his exploration of the music of Bach and Handel

*Example III–8*

Quae-ri - te pri - mum    reg - num    De - - - - -

etc.

etc.

etc.

(see p. 55)

- - i        et

*Example III–9*

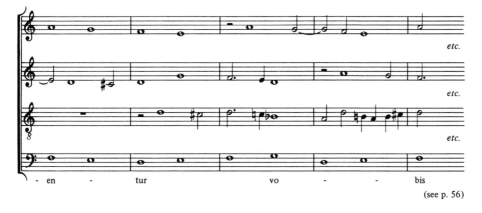

(see p. 56)

during the same decade. His interest in polyphony continued to deepen at a time that was also marked by his most intense pedagogical activity, and in the course of instruction he designed for Attwood we find a first, classical, presentation of what was to become the standard for later ages—harmony, counterpoint, and studies in contemporary forms.

It is interesting that this course of studies shows such reserve with regard to fugal instruction. The "school fugue" was not as yet the established norm that it became by the time the young Beethoven commenced his studies. Mozart was more concerned with the ubiquitous fugal manner that had guided his own training than with examples of fugal form, and the spirit of Martini's correction is readily apparent in the most famous didactic example to have come down to us in his hand: the revision of a minuet for string quartet that Attwood submitted to him during the later part of his studies.

Mozart had probably written out the first eight measures of the melody. He had used this method with an earlier, less gifted student, the daughter of the Duke of Guines, as we know from the postscript of a letter to his father (May 14, 1778):

She has no ideas; no thought comes to her. I have tried whatever I could—among other things I took to the device of writing down a very simple minuet to see if she could invent a variation. Alas, it was in vain. Now it occurred to me that she was only at a loss of how to start. I began to vary the first measure and told her to continue along the same lines. This worked after a fashion, and when she had finally finished, I asked her to take up a new melody—no more than the beginning of the top part. Well, she deliberated for a quarter of an hour—yet nothing came forth. In the end I wrote four measures of a minuet and said to her: "Look, what a fool I am; I have started a minuet and cannot even complete the first section—be so good as to help me out." And she thought that was totally impossible.

Mozart's father answered:

You write me that you have given the Duke's young girl her fourth lesson, and you want her to produce ideas—do you think everyone has your genius?

More sophisticated is the principle of assignment that appears in a draft Mozart prepared for Attwood (Example III–10). The latter, in turn, seems to have applied this principle to some extent in the minuet mentioned above (see p. 61): he used the opening of the first violin part in the continuation of the second violin part, and he retained the melodic line Mozart had written for the first eight measures. In all other respects, however, the minuet under discussion seems to be entirely Attwood's composition. He must have decided to work with melodic material he was able to derive from the beginning and with motifs at which he had arrived in working out the accompaniment.

Mozart went through the finished version, added a natural sign where it had been forgotten, and rewrote a passage to avoid parallel octaves, but then he started afresh and wrote a completely new version. As his own teacher had done fifteen years earlier, he followed the student's conception; in fact, he took over the outline of the piece completely. He "merely" loosened the four-part fabric while he tightened its thought.

Attwood took the manuscript of his studies back to England where it was eventually bequeathed to John Goss, his student and successor as organist at St. Paul's. Goss published the two versions of the minuet in his *Introduction to Harmony and Thoroughbass* (1833), and they appeared in several reprints. One of them, contained in a volume entitled *Chamber Music* (1913) by Thomas Dunhill, Professor of Harmony and Counterpoint at the Royal College of Music, bears the annotation, adapted from a Shakespeare quotation, that the original was transformed "into something strange and wonderful."

*Example III–10*

# Classical Studies in Polyphony

*Examples of Fugues from* Gradus ad Parnassum
*annotated by Haydn*

Fugue in A

Lic: non bona
(Haydn)

53

Fugue in C

*Mozart's Test Piece*
*Mozart's Version*

Quae-ri - te pri - mum  re - gnum  De - - -

- i  et ju - sti - ti - am e - jus, et

haec o - mni - a  ad - ji - ci - en - tur

vo - bis. Al - le - lu - ja!

*Mozart's Test Piece*
*Martini's Version*

Quae-ri - te pri - mum　　reg - num　De　—　—　i

et　ju - sti - ti - am　e　—　ius, et　haec　om -

ni - a　ad - ji - ci - en - tur_____　vo -

- bis　al - le - lu - ja.

*Examples of Fugues from the Attwood Studies*
*annotated by Mozart*

Fugue in F

(Mozart)

Fugue in G

Fugue in F

(Mozart)

(Mozart)

*Minuet from the Attwood Studies*
*Attwood's Version*

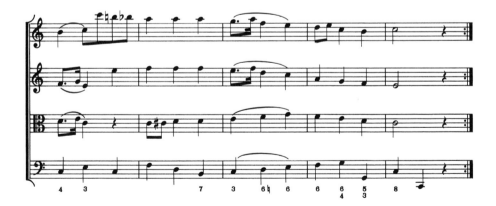

*Mozart's Version*

# ·IV·

# Beethoven and Schubert

As we view the documentation of the master-artisan relationship in the eighteenth century, the role of the great composer turns from teacher to student, and the emphasis in the teaching process shifts from freely applied polyphonic training to strict contrapuntal study. The most eminent, and controversial, student was Beethoven, but the account of Beethoven's studies must be seen against the larger background of the development of eighteenth century instruction in species counterpoint.

There is a surprising contradiction in the text of C.P.E. Bach's letter quoted at the beginning of this volume. His categoric distinction between "*dry species* of counterpoint" and "what was practical" is followed by a list of the ten composers whom his father held in particularly high esteem during his last years, and this list begins with Fux. Similar contradictons are contained in the annotations for the *Gradus* translation which Bach's student Lorenz Christoph Mizler published in Leipzig, probably at Bach's prompting. What both Bach's son and his student overlooked was the fact that to Bach, as to Fux, the contrapuntal species continued to represent "what was practical." In their deliberate rhythmic and melodic design they were akin to the traditional *solfeggiamenti*—exercises for instruction in singing—and to the "divisions" applied so widely in the early instrumental literature and still reflected in the arrangement of Handel's first group of thoroughbass examples.

Contrary to general opinion, the contrapuntal species had kept their place in the practice of composition, and Christoph Wolff has drawn attention to Bach's use of the third contrapuntal species in the *Credo* of the B-minor Mass and to his similarly consistent application of the fourth contrapuntal species elsewhere.[1] This phenomenon is emphasized in the *Credo* setting through the reappearance of the *cantus firmus* in its original sense—Gregorian chant; we find it in comparable examples throughout Handel's choral work and even in the theme formation of the finales for Mozart's String Quartet K. 387 and the Jupiter Symphony. Mozart's Divertimento for string trio, composed one month after the

---

[1] *Der Stile Antico in der Musik Johann Sebastian Bachs* (Wiesbaden, 1968), p. 68.

symphony, pays the most remarkable homage to the practice of strict counterpoint. The theme of its variation movement is reduced at its last exposure to a veritable *cantus firmus* introduced in the viola part and accompanied in the two other instrumental parts by running passages which clearly suggest the second and third counterpoint species.

There is no question that Mozart's teaching activity influenced his writing in such instances. His interest in strict counterpoint as a pedagogic device had grown during his Vienna years, and the last of the preserved study books of Mozart students, that of Franz Jacob Freystädtler, shows that Mozart's instruction now began with species counterpoint and remained limited to it, although in a course of studies that is a model of thoroughness. A crisis arose when the first student of overwhelming talent was faced with such a challenge, and this characterized the teacher-student relationship of Haydn and Beethoven.

As we know, Beethoven had intended to study with Mozart, and he had gone to Vienna for this purpose in 1787. But the leave he was granted from his employment at the electoral court in Bonn was too short, and when he was able to return, several years later, Mozart had died. Beethoven therefore decided to study with Haydn. The awkward implication of second choice was voiced in the famous farewell message Beethoven had received from his friend and patron, Count Waldstein:

Through unremitting hard work you shall receive the spirit of Mozart from Haydn's hands.[2]

What he did receive was doubtless the kind of training to which Mozart would have subjected him and which is amply documented in the Attwood and Freystädtler studies from the very same years. Curiously, Beethoven considered the systematic instruction in counterpoint he obtained from Haydn not thorough enough, and in the course of his studies he turned to other Viennese composers.

Much has been written about Haydn's "failure" as a teacher of Beethoven, but it no more than confirms the difficulty of grasping the complexity of the two artistic personalities involved. Against the rash conjectures of posterity stands a record of the mutual regard in which the two composers held each other (Beethoven's carefully kept expense book contains the charming entry of 22 *Kreuzer* spent on hot chocolate "für haidn und mich"). In fact, stylistic analysis has shown that in time the older learned from the younger master, as the student had learned from the teacher.

When Beethoven published his piano sonatas Opus 2, dedicated to Haydn, he was twenty-six years old—the same age at which Mozart began the composition of his six quartets dedicated to Haydn. While the association of Beethoven and Haydn cannot be compared to that of Mozart and Haydn, we must not dismiss the fact that Haydn's student was a composer of some experience, whose Opus 1 had been preceded by a number of other published works available in European markets. Yet Beethoven's impatience at perfecting his technique was prompted by more than the personal disposition of a brusque young artist of proven competence whose wish for undisturbed study had been all too long postponed. There was, both in Beethoven's own attitude and that of his generation, a new sense of inquiry, a new critical orientation towards the past.

[2] Anton Felix Schindler, *Beethoven as I Knew Him*, ed. Donald W. MacArdle, trans. Constance S. Jolly (New York, 1972), p. 48.

Haydn acquainted Beethoven with the study of modes that had been much debated throughout the eighteenth century, and when Beethoven took up lessons with Johann Georg Albrechtsberger at the time of Haydn's second departure for London—probably at Haydn's recommendation—Beethoven temporarily abandoned this study. Albrechtsberger's *Gründliche Anweisung zu Komposition* (1790) stands as the classic treatise in which the discipline of counterpoint was first reduced to the modern scales of major and minor, and in becoming Albrechtsberger's student, Beethoven returned to the beginning of two-part counterpoint according to the new system. But when Beethoven compiled notes for the instruction of his own student, Archduke Rudolph, twenty years later, he seems to have fully realized the problem of separating the technique from its historical basis; he went back to modal counterpoint and the teaching of Haydn.

The handwriting of Haydn joins that of Beethoven on the fifty-four-page manuscript entitled *Übungen im Contrapunkt* that formed the basis of Beethoven's polyphonic training. The fact that Beethoven provided this title on a separate page, that he designated as "Exercises in Counterpoint" a collection of pages written with, for him, unusual care, helps to explain the nature of the manuscript: these pages do not represent the examples Beethoven wrote down day by day as he prepared his lessons, but a fair copy in which he gathered groups of already existing exercises from a number that may have been considerably larger—though not corrected. This fact is corroborated by some recognizable gaps, the extent of which we can estimate in view of the total design, and in particular by one example—the last on page *33*—in which Beethoven made an obvious copying mistake.[3] This example, like all the others, shows Beethoven writing a counterpoint (in this case in half notes) on an assigned *cantus firmus*. But instead of following the typical study method of copying out the *cantus firmus* first and then adding the contrapuntal lines, he proceeded the other way round, copying the counterpoint in half notes first, from what must have been an earlier draft. In doing so, he skipped a measure and, when he subsequently added the *cantus firmus*, recognized his error (as he was about to write a passage in parallel fifths). He tried to mend it, but as the copy became illegible, crossed out the whole example and started it anew on the next page (Example IV–1).[4]

Beethoven's *Übungen im Contrapunkt* was among a large number of autographs sold after the composer's death to his Viennese publisher Tobias Haslinger, and the collection was still in its original folder when the Beethoven scholar Gustav Nottebohm subjected it to critical review forty-five years later. Nottebohm found it in a group of folders containing Beethoven's studies with Albrechtsberger and numerous related writings. He recognized at the outset that there were some entries in the manuscript which were written by neither Beethoven nor Haydn but Albrechtsberger.

Evidently Beethoven had taken along the fair copy of his studies with Haydn when he commenced studies with Albrechtsberger, and the latter tried to acquaint himself with the precise state of Beethoven's training. The first of the annotations that Albrechtsberger

---

[3] Numbers in Italics *(1–54)* refer to the pagination of Beethoven's *Übungen im Contrapunkt* beginning on p. 87 below.

[4] Both versions, given here in their original form, were subjected to changes. Beethoven tried to correct the copying mistake in the first, and Haydn corrected a mistake in the second (cf. facsimile no. *33*).

*Example IV–1*

Faulty copy (original version)

(see fac. *33*)

Corrected copy (original version)

[sic]

(see fac. *34*)

made is the word "gut"—his comment on the use of the cambiata figure—at the bottom of page *4*. (The second note of the measure may have been changed by Albrechtsberger in order to apply the cambiata, but it is evident from the preceding example that Beethoven was familiar with it; Haydn had used it also in one of his corrections on p. *18*.) At the right hand upper corner of the next page, he commented further on this device, demonstrating its use first in an upper voice, with the added entries "WN:" (for "Wechselnote," the German equivalent of cambiata) and "oben" (above), and then in a lower voice, with the added entry "unten die 4$^{te}$ in die 6" (below, the fourth resolving into the sixth).

On the last system of the same page appears one more remark that belongs in the same context and applies to an instance in which the cambiata is undesirable ("übel") because it would involve the tritone ("mi-fa") within a melodic line ("in einer Stimme"). Thus it would have to be judged differently from the passage marked "gut" on the preceding page (crosses centered in the margin refer the entries to one another). Albrechtsberger then continues the discussion of the tritone with three brief examples that show its use distributed over two melodic lines. In the first and last of these he indicates the tritone again as "mi-fa," and he marks the first and second examples as good and again good ("gut"—"auch gut"). But the last example is designated "übel; weil zwey vollkommene Accorde aufein-ander folgen" (bad because two successive perfect consonances are involved).

   Albrechtsberger's remarks are concluded on page 6 of Beethoven's manuscript. In the cadence of the first example, Albrechtsberger writes "Lic:" (license) to denote another tritone, occurring between the upper voice and the *cantus firmus*. At the left margin he offers a fuller explanation for such use of the tritone in the Aeolian and Phrygian modes ("A moll" and "E plagal"), and this annotation, finally, is connected with two passages he writes out at the bottom of the page, one marked "Etwas aus A moll" (something in A Minor) and the other representing a corresponding example in the Phrygian mode. The connection between the marginalia at the side and at the bottom of the page was intended to be made with the customary "vi—de" annotation; Albrechtsberger, however, entered only the first of the two syllables ("vi") and omitted the second, though its place is marked by an asterisk corresponding to the one noted next to "vi." The full text of Albrechtsber-ger's comment reads:

> h a      ist ein
> f __       erlaubtes
>
> Mi contra Fa
> en A moll und
> E plagal
>             vi
>
> in den trans-
>             x weichen
> ponierten x            Tonarten
>
> fällt dieses Mi
> contra Fa auch
> auf den 6$^{\text{ten}}$ Ton
> der unteren
> Stim͞e

(The line above the last word is a customary symbol used here and elsewhere in the text indicating that the consonant is to be doubled; see page 6).

> b a      is a
> f __       permissible
>
> Mi against Fa
> in A Minor and
> E plagal
>             vi

in the trans-
x       minor
posed x       keys

this Mi
against Fa occurs additionally
on the 6ᵗʰ degree
placed in the lower
voice.

One gathers that Beethoven was in good hands, although Albrechtsberger's methodical approach eventually proved too much for him.

While Nottebohm's achievement in reconstructing the original order from a bewildering array that had gone through various unreliable interpretations was remarkable, he misunderstood the very nature of the manuscript embodying Beethoven's studies with Haydn. It was a summary that must have been preceded by more detailed studies and that was summarily reviewed—possibly in no more than two or three sessions. Nottebohm was puzzled by the "strictness and refinement" with which Haydn had corrected some portions and the entire lack of correction in others, and he reached the conclusion that Haydn was "not fully familiar with the requirements and peculiarities of strict counterpoint." This judgement is all the more surprising since Nottebohm had at his disposal Haydn's personal copy of Fux's *Gradus* with its incredible wealth of annotations.

Faced with a manuscript that he could not fully understand, the scholar turned counterpoint teacher (he was a student of Mendelssohn and Schumann and had received contrapuntal training from Simon Sechter) and from the didactic perspective of his time, marked Beethoven's as well as Haydn's mistakes.

There is a curious interest in spotting the mistakes of great composers (and the reader may sense it again in going through the facsimile reproduction of Beethoven's exercises). But while Nottebohm was unquestionably right in pointing out parallel fifths and octaves, he was on less secure ground in his censure of other passages. He was clearly out of his domain in criticizing such matters at Haydn's failure to use the leading tone as the penultimate note of a counterpoint (Example IV–2) or Haydn's use of the unprepared seventh.

There are two fundamental problems involved. One is that the discipline of strict

*Example IV–2*

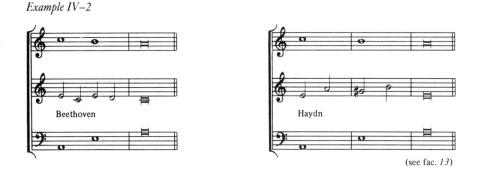

(see fac. *13*)

counterpoint had not only become rare in the Classic era but also, in the teaching of Haydn and Mozart, had undergone definite changes—their era was as removed from that of Fux as Fux's had been from that of Palestrina, his professed model. The other problem is that Haydn proceeded in a manner which shows that he was quite conscious of the value of his advice to the young composer: elementary flaws he may have left to the student's own review, but in intricate problems of part-writing he was generous with his comment; he directed his special attention to a choice of problems. Nowhere is this shown more convincingly than on one page of Beethoven's studies that deals with the difficult assignment of introducing suspensions into the texture of four independently moving parts. The details of a single page show Haydn's watchful concern for pure four-part sound and his deftness in restoring it (see page *45*). Similarly, he chose the four-part exercises for some of his most sensitive corrections of Beethoven's melodic lines (Example IV–3).

Conversely, the earlier pages of Beethoven's studies contain next to nothing in the way of Haydn's corrections, with one notable exception: in forming the final cadence in the Phrygian mode, to which Beethoven was totally unaccustomed, Haydn realized that the student needed the teacher's help, and his corrections are comprehensive, lending more

*Example IV–3*

spaciousness, both with regard to motion and sonority, to the three-part texture (see p. *7*).

Nottebohm had not taken into account the fact that Haydn had deliberately altered some of Fux's examples (as had Mozart). And as it turned out, Haydn was justified in the premise that Beethoven might assume a similarly critical attitude without explicit guidance. This throws some light on the aspect of contrapuntal technique which Nottebohm found more confusing than any other in judging Beethoven's studies with Haydn—hidden fifths and octaves.

Nottebohm pointed out that Haydn had corrected such passages in Beethoven's examples but in doing so, had fallen into the same mistake (Example IV–4). He did not point out, however, that with the hidden octaves Haydn wrote in correcting Beethoven's hidden fifths, the passage was changed so that the hidden parallels no longer involved an outer part but only inner parts and that the distribution of similar and contrary motion between all parts was more evenly balanced than before.

*Example IV–4*

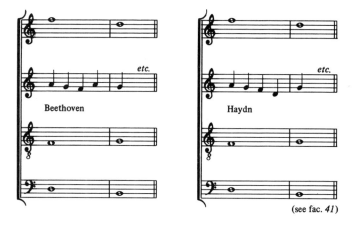

(see fac. *41*)

Nottebohm remarks that in one instance Haydn corrected Beethoven's use of hidden fifths even though the same hidden fifths occur in Fux's examples, and he failed to come to grips with the fact that we are dealing here with a matter of opinion, not rule. We have, in fact, Beethoven's own later comments on a discussion which Fux offers in connection with one of the models he gives for the third contrapuntal species in four-part writing (Example IV–5). Fux had placed the letters A and B in his example to mark the hidden octaves and fifths which, as he says, "need not be considered a mistake because of the difficulty of this species." Beethoven adds: "Such liberties are more acceptable in a descending than in an ascending motion" (referring to point A); but with regard to point B he writes "the latter would never be excusable for my ear." (Haydn, somewhat more objectively, had noted in his marginal remarks "Male juxta alios authores"—bad, according to other authors).[5]

---

[5] Haydn used Latin in his annotations of Fux's Latin text.

*Example IV–5*

When Beethoven, years later, compiled his own teaching material for the instruction of Archduke Rudolph, he added one of his typical asides:

Dear Friends, I took such trouble merely in order to clarify bass figuration so I might guide others. So far as mistakes are concerned, I almost never needed to study for myself; I felt such sensitivity since childhood that I proceeded without knowing that something had to be so or could not be otherwise.

It is relatively easy to obtain a clear view of the course of Beethoven's work with Haydn, when one understands the highly systematic design of the manuscript. Haydn had assigned Beethoven six *cantus firmi* which he had freely adapted from those given in Fux's *Gradus ad Parnassum* (Example IV–6). They are taken up in the order of the six

*Example IV–6*

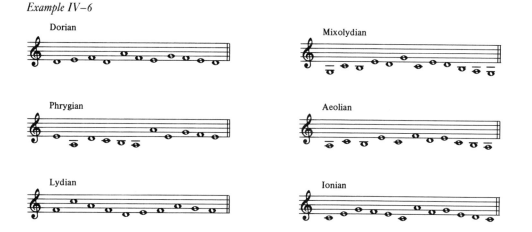

authentic modes, in two-, three-, and four-part counterpoint respectively, and the sections

into which the manuscript is thus divided are, with some exceptions, marked by Beethoven
with superscriptions:

2 stimiger Contrapunkt
Nota Contra Notam
(Two-part counterpoint
Note against note)
[page *2*]

2^te Gattung des zweistimigen C
(Second species of two-part counterpoint)
[page *3*]

3^te Gattung des zweistimigen C.
[page *4*]

4^te Gattung des zweistimigen C.
[page *6*]

3 stimiger Contrapunkt
[page *7*]

2^te Gattung des 3 stimigen C.
[page *10*]

3^te Gattung des 3 stimigen C,
[page *15*]

4^te Gattung des 3 stimigen C.
[page *19*]

4 stimiger Contrapunkt
[page *24*]

As we can gather, the exercises are arranged according to the order of Fux's contrapuntal species. The fact that there is no heading for the fifth species in the two-part examples is due to one of the major gaps in the manuscript: no two-part examples in this species
are included, although a number that might have been planned in accordance with the
number of examples in the other species can be calculated. In the three-part examples, a
similar lack signifies a further gap, but in four-part counterpoint, Beethoven omitted the
headings for all species.

The number of examples chosen for each species also follows a strict plan. There is
one example each for every contrapuntal situation: one upper and one lower counterpoint
is provided for each *cantus firmus* in two parts, one counterpoint each for the three registers

in three parts, and one counterpoint each for the four registers in four parts.[6] In the exceptional cases where Beethoven wrote two examples instead of one in a given constellation, he numbered them, as a rule, 1) and 2); the last of the three-part examples in the fourth species (page *22*) is marked 1) but is not followed by a corresponding second example—indicating once again a gap in the manuscript. A schematic design for the course of studies can thus be given, as follows:

| | Modes: | D | E | F | G | A | C | pages |
|---|---|---|---|---|---|---|---|---|
| | 1st species | 4 | 2 | 2 | 2 | 2 | 2 | *2–3* |
| | 2nd species | 2 | 2 | 2 | 2 | 2 | 2 | *3–4* |
| Examples of two-part | 3rd species | 2 | 2 | 2 | 2 | 2 | 2 | *4–5* |
| counterpoint | 4th species | 2 | 2 | 2 | 2 | 2 | – | *6* |
| | 5th species | – | – | – | – | – | – | |
| | | | | | | | | |
| | 1st species | 2 | 4 | 2 | 2 | 2 | 2 | *7–10* |
| Examples of three-part | 2nd species | 3 | 3 | 4 | 3 | 3 | 4 | *10–14* |
| counterpoint | 3rd species | 3 | 3 | 3 | 3 | 3 | 3 | *15–19* |
| | 4th species | 3 | 3 | 3 | 4 | 1 | – | *19–22* |
| | 5th species | – | – | – | – | 3 | 3 | *23–24* |
| | | | | | | | | |
| | 1st species | 4 | 4 | 4+1[7] | 4 | 4 | 4 | *24–30* |
| Examples of four-part | 2nd species | 4 | 4 | 4 | 4 | 4 | 4 | *30–36* |
| counterpoint | 3rd species | 4 | 4 | 4 | 4 | 4 | 3 | *36–42* |
| | 4th species | 4 | 5 | 4 | 4 | 4 | 5 | *42–48* |
| | 5th species | 4 | 4 | 4 | 4 | 4 | 4 | *49–54* |

The earliest part of the volume shows no corrections except for minor changes Beethoven seems to have made while copying, as he apparently did throughout the manuscript. Albrechtsberger's notes begin with the third species of two-part counterpoint and extend into the fourth; examples for the fifth species are missing.

Haydn's comments begin with three-part counterpoint, prompted by the difficulties Beethoven was having—as did the student in the dialogue section of Fux's text—in writing the Phrygian cadence. These comments are concerned with questions of hidden parallels and a full three-part sound, and they cover the first three species. The fourth and fifth species are again without corrections, except for those made by Beethoven himself. Entries made by Haydn resume with the beginning of the four-part examples and continue through all the species, with particular concentration upon two issues: the improvement of the melodic line in quarter note motion and the clarity of four-part sound obtained by avoiding anticipation and duplication of chord tones in the resolution of tied dissonances.

[6] In order to save space and copying effort, Beethoven arranged his two-part exercises in systems that seem to combine three parts, but in reality each system contains two examples, one for an upper and one for a lower counterpoint written on the same *cantus firmus* (Mozart's students had used the same method in their respective manuscripts).

[7] An alternate version for the first example on page *27* appears on the same four-stave system.

The most striking instances of Haydn's corrections have been discussed in the pre-
vious pages, as have Albrechtsberger's additions to the manuscript; further corrections in
the manuscript are covered in the commentary (below, pp. 87 ff) for the respective facsimile pages. That not all of them can definitely be ascribed to Haydn or to Beethoven himself
is due to the fact that in its early state the manuscript went through several hands. We
know, for instance, that before submitting it to Albrechtsberger, Beethoven had shown it
to the Viennese composer Johann Schenk, who had studied with a pupil of Fux. Beethoven's gratitude for Schenk's advice has been recorded in the memoirs of Anton Schindler,
Beethoven's close associate in later years; but in the end the manuscript shows no critical
changes that cannot be attributed to Haydn's hand.

Beethoven's studies direct our attention finally to another figure who played a dominant role in the music of the Imperial capital: Antonio Salieri. Viennese Classicism, which
in the historical view is an age categorically defined beyond question, was in many ways a
transitional period. It was characteristic of Viennese musical life at the end of the eighteenth century that its leadership was divided between two offices representing different
styles: even before Fux's day, the musical directorship at St. Stephan's had been in the
hands of German-Austrians, whereas the musical directorship at court remained predominantly Italian. While Albrechtsberger was chapelmaster at St. Stephan's, Salieri served
as court composer, primarily concerned with opera; but he was also responsible for training the choristers of the Imperial chapel. The most illustrious of his young singers was
Franz Schubert.

Within a span of ten years both Beethoven and Schubert were students of Salieri, and
while their teacher-pupil relationships were altogether different, the preserved studies, in
both cases written on texts by Metastasio, show a remarkable overlap. Beethoven had
turned to Salieri in order to gain experience in Italian vocal composition, a field that had
remained foreign to him. It was just as foreign to the young Schubert, and although he
never showed any genuine involvement, he was obliged to pursue the same manner of
studies that Beethoven had undertaken before him. It is fascinating to compare their manuscripts.

What renders Schubert's studies in Italian vocal composition particularly interesting
is that they reflect two entirely different worlds in the writings of student and teacher.
Though Salieri's hand provided sure guidance—which Schubert seems to have fully appre-
ciated—the maturing language of the pupil transcended the comprehension of the master.
It was the truly Schubertian phrase that met with Salieri's criticism (Example IV–7).
While his suggestions invariably show his competence in vocal declamation, his understanding ceased when it came to the incipient dissolution of a harmonic idiom guided
strictly by tonal function. Thus he changed a number of similar passages (Examples IV–8
and IV–9). But these instances mark a very late phase of Schubert's studies with Salieri,
and do not point to the real problem that arose in the course of the instruction.

Schubert began his professional career, like Haydn, as a Viennese choirboy. He was
accepted into the Imperial Chapel when he was eleven years old at the recommendation of
Salieri, and the chapelmaster soon singled him out for individual instruction in composi-

*Example IV–7*

*Example IV–8*

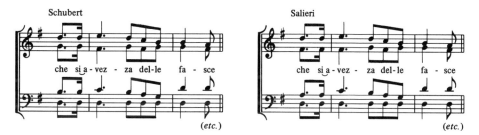

*Example IV–9*

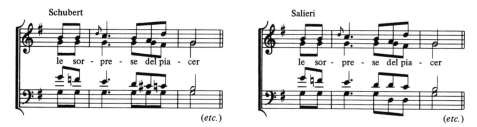

tion. Schubert's formal training began with a course in strict counterpoint not unlike that which Beethoven had undertaken as Haydn's student. It is clear from the preserved exercises, however, that Salieri followed the "modern" method of Albrechtsberger whose *Gründliche Anweisung zur Komposition*, published in 1790, may have served, directly or indirectly, as a textbook. Like Mozart and Haydn, but unlike Albrechtsberger, Salieri does not seem to have subscribed to the concept of organized fugal training, and it was this subject that held Schubert's foremost interest.

Apparently the only fugue that Schubert wrote under Salieri's direction was a brief two-part study that remained incomplete, though what is lost would likely not have amounted to more than a few measures. After the initial exercises in two-, three-, and four-part counterpoint, Salieri had given the student some assignments in imitation in which one or two subjects are carried through two voices in strict canon and concluded with a cadence.

The two-part fugue is similar to these studies and may have been written in connection with them. It contains a few corrections by Salieri which stress on the one hand, the singable quality of the theme and on the other, the melodic integrity of its chosen form (Example IV–10). Schubert's versions show greater emphasis upon canonic play, but on the whole, Salieri does not take exception to Schubert's frequent use of canonic-motivic technique. The canonic answers of the theme produce, in fact, the typical problem of harmonic fugal structure: the canonic answer on the dominant leads the harmonic design unavoidably to the dominant of the dominant. Thus as early as this, Schubert met with a problem that was to occupy him throughout his life—the problem of fugal answer. He continued to deal with it in extended studies in four-part fugal writing, ostensibly undertaken without Salieri's supervision. The first of them shows the dilemma to its full extent. Schubert had chosen a theme that moved sequentially down from the fifth to the first

*Example IV–10*

degree of the key. With three subsequent extrances, each at the lower fifth of the preceding one, Schubert obtained a set of fugal answers that took the exposition straight through the circle of fifths, from G major to B♭ major (Example IV–11).

A remarkable process now took place. The inexperienced student of fugue, dissatisfied with the lack of tonal stability, rewrote the exposition with alternating entrances in the tonic and dominant keys (Example IV–12). We can be quite sure that this was not done at Salieri's prompting, because Salieri would not have tolerated the repeated use of the unsupported fourth (a point he had made a number of times in Schubert's earlier counterpoint exercises). Schubert pasted the new version over the old and crossed out two measures written in bringing about their connection. Although he had re-established the original key of G major, he retained the modulatory sequences leading to B♭ major because

*Example IV–11*

*Example IV–12*

he was evidently intrigued with the combination of keys related by a third. He continued the sequential imitations even to reach E♭ major and balanced the entire section against a later one that leads from the major third below the original key to the major third above it, B major. Although the harmonic experimenting resulted in a structural design marked by great skill, the entire fugue, with its abundant motivic work, retains a decidedly academic character. Schubert's own hand can be recognized only in the final pedal-point passage, which is based on the elaboration of a motif at which he had arrived in the last modulation of the first exposition (Example IV–13).

*Example IV–13*

Schubert pursued the problem of fugal answer in a number of other four-part examples in which he tried to work with the chromatic "codetta" that he had introduced in his correction of the exposition in the G-major fugue. We can observe in these works a steady growth of fugal technique, but he never fully solved its problems. This becomes clear from Schubert's compositions over the next ten years. Even the fugue in the *Wandererfantasie* contains a curiously interpolated measure, written to enable the composer to return to the original key in the initial exposition.

It was not until Schubert worked on revisions in his A♭ major Mass, begun in the same year as the *Wandererfantasie*, that he supplanted a fugal exposition written with canonic real answers by one employing tonal answers (the concluding fugue of the *Gloria*).

Two years later, in 1824, Schubert's brother Ferdinand mentions in a letter to the composer that he had dispatched the requested fugues by Bach (a copy of the *Well-Tempered Clavier*). In the same year Anton Schindler recorded a remark made by Schubert to the effect that he wished to turn to Simon Sechter for renewed contrapuntal studies in which "his old master Salieri had left perceptible gaps." We have mentioned the story of Schubert's lesson with Sechter, and what remains to be added here is a fuller explanation of the striking encounter as well as its documentation.

Composers of Schubert's generation were no longer naturally versed in the imitative exposition of thematic material and required historical guidance on this point. Sechter, later the teacher of Liszt and Bruckner and himself trained in the Albrechtsberger school, was the leading Viennese theorist and doubtless the logical person to consult. He was working at that time on a new edition of the *Manual of Fugue* (1753–1754) by Friedrich Wilhelm Marpurg, the theorist who had discussed matters of fugal technique in conversa-

tion with Bach, and we can recognize signs of Marpurg's work in Schubert's lesson with
Sechter.

The incident which sparked Schubert's decision to communicate with Sechter is well
recorded. Schubert's unabating interest in fugal technique had led him to compose an
unusual work, a fugue for organ in a four-hand setting that was written a few months
before his death. The occasion was an excursion which the composer undertook with a
friend to visit the monastery of Heiligenkreuz, south of Vienna, whose church had a
renowned organ. In a friendly contest, they had arranged that each of them would write a
fugue to test the famous instrument, and both works were published shortly thereafter,
Schubert's fugue as Op. posth. 152.

Schubert had chosen a theme closely related to that of the F♯-minor fugue from Book
I of the *Well-Tempered Clavier*. While the work is one of the wonders of Schubert's late
style, its exposition proved, once more, troublesome, and in order to bring about a modulation which would return to the initial key with sufficient ease, Schubert subjected it to
several revisions. We can recognize three stages in the working process. The first can still
be seen in the version subsequently published, with which Schubert had remained dissatisfied, and it was evidently this problematical fugal exposition that contributed to Schubert's resolve now to seek Sechter's advice (Example IV–14).

*Example IV–14*

When the manuscript of Schubert's lesson with Sechter was discovered recently, it
became clear that another Schubert autograph, which had been known but not fully interpreted, was a rough draft Schubert had written in preparation for the lesson. It contains a
number of two-part fugal expositions sketched for the obvious purpose of setting forth the
questions that had been on Schubert's mind regarding the matter of fugal answer. The
first of these shows the beginning of the organ fugue in a revised version (Example IV–

15). A third version, finally, appears in the fair copy Schubert wrote to submit to Sechter (Example IV–16).

In the course of these three versions, Schubert eliminates the rests that stress the modulatory deviations and reverts from the emphasis on the dominant key to that on the tonic in a more connected flow of voices leading to the point where a third entrance can occur in the original key. This, the perfect balance of tonic and dominant in the thematic exposition was the central issue, and it became the subject of the lesson.

Schubert had numbered the examples he drafted, assigning a new number to each pair; however, the numbers do not refer to their sequence but to the degrees of the major and minor scales on which the fugal themes begin. This system corresponds indeed to Marpurg's method which—following Jean Philippe Rameau's *Traité d'harmonie* (1722)—

*Example IV–15*

*Example IV–16*

(see p. 143)

presents the rules for fugal answer with specific reference to the tones on which fugal
themes begin and end. Marpurg's principal rule is that tonic and dominant must represent
complete correspondence in the fugal exposition (the unavoidably uneven division of the
octave into a larger tonic and a smaller dominant segment necessitates variants in the shape
of thematic statements giving rise to the tonal answer). Thus when the beginning or the
end of a fugal theme—and at times other salient points of its melodic line—are determined
by the tonic triad, the answer must contain corresponding tones of the dominant triad,
and vice versa.

Sechter's corrections are guided by this rule. In Schubert's first example he shows
two possible adjustments of the theme in the answer, first by changing the end of the
theme and then—notated above the system—by changing the beginning of the theme
(Example IV–17). In Schubert's second pair of examples, Sechter seeks to clarify the tonic

*Example IV–17*

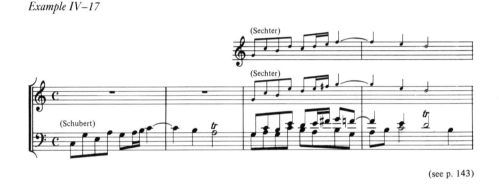

(see p. 143)

and dominant functions, respectively, by a brief anticipation of the opening interval skip
(Example IV–18). In the third pair of examples, he adds the word "jonisch" (Ionian) to a

*Example IV–18*

(see p. 144)

correction which may have been entered by Schubert himself. As indicated by Sechter's
later annotations, this applies to a fugal answer kept strictly within the confines of the
modal scale, reaching the first degree at a point analogous to that at which the theme
reaches the fifth—an earlier explanation of the tonal answer. Sechter completes the version
thus designated at the margin, and he adds for comparison the version arriving not at the
first but at the second degree; in this case the answer exceeds the basic scale and thus does

not qualify as tonal (Example IV–19). In the second fugal exposition of the fourth pair of examples, finally, Sechter apparently changed the first note from d to e—once again, to clarify the tonic-dominant relationship of theme and answer (Example IV–20).

*Example IV–19*

(see p. 144)

*Example IV–20*

(see p. 145)

The principle governing Sechter's corrections is fully illustrated in a series of examples he wrote out on an additional page. In a basic design he presents a theme consisting of the tonic and dominant tones only, and inverts this scheme with its countermelody to obtain the tonal answer (Example IV–21). Next, rather than following Marpurg's somewhat cumbersome method of discussing fugal themes beginning on successive degrees of the scale, he uses a series of themes whose stepwise increasing, predominantly linear, melodic contours are faithfully duplicated in real answers.

*Example IV–21*

(see p. 147)

Arrived at the ambitus of the octave, Sechter returns to the explanation of the tonal answer which he describes, as before, by the word "jonisch," thus alluding to the origin of the concept in modal practice. In contradistinction, he designates the real answer as new ("neu") because it moves beyond the tones of the basic scale. Then he gives an example for the tonal answer in a minor key, pointing out, however, that the linear use of the minor scale will lend itself again to the real answer, and he sketches a theme in A minor whose answer, accordingly, would be transferred to E minor ("ins E moll") by a transposition whose strict degree scheme he indicates for both theme and answer (Example IV–22).

*Example IV–22*

(see p. 148)

   The assignment of a three-part fugue, whose exposition Sechter outlines, forms a
moving gesture with which he concludes the lesson. In tribute to his incomparable student,
the chromatic theme is drawn from the letters of his name (omitting those that cannot be
interpreted as letters of the scale): S (e♭), c, h (b♮), b (b♭), e (Example IV–23). "We had had
but a single lesson . . ." Sechter wrote later in a letter to Ferdinand Luib, editor of the
*Allgemeine Wiener Musik-Zeitung*, who had asked Sechter for biographical details; ". . . scarcely
nine days passed and Schubert had died." Shortly after Schubert's death, Sechter pub-

*Example IV–23*

lished a fugue dedicated to his memory in which he had carried out the assignment given to the composer (see pp. 149 ff). The serious intent of the smoothly written work cannot fail to affect the listener, but it marks a critical moment in didactic history, and we must consider it a fortunate turn in tragic circumstances that the discussion of teacher and student never entered the domain of true composition.

# Beethoven's Studies with Haydn

## Counterpoint

*1*

Beethoven writes Übüngen for Übungen in the title.

2

---

*TWO-PART COUNTERPOINT*
Two examples on the *cantus firmus* in D
Two examples on the *cantus firmus* in D
Two examples on the *cantus firmus* in E
Two examples on the *cantus firmus* in F
Two examples on the *cantus firmus* in G

The part containing the *cantus firmus* is regularly marked "c.f." here and subsequently. The second pair of examples forms an exception representing variants of the first (and marked 2); the corresponding 1) appears amidst the heading *Nota contra Notam*.

An alternate note e is entered in pencil, apparently by Beethoven, in the third measure of the last system.

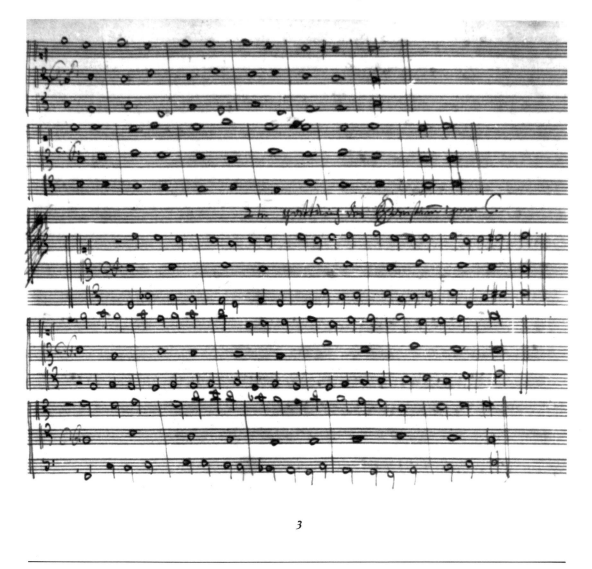

3

*4*

All corrections, here and throughout the two-part exercises, are apparently in Beethoven's hand. Albrechtberger's marginal text begins on this page; he enters a cross and the word "gut" under the bottom line (cf. p. 66), probably referring to a change entered directly above. A similar change in the preceding measure is clarified by the letter g.

5

---

*Two examples on a cantus firmus* in F, with marginal remarks by Albrechtsberger (see p. 66).
Two examples on the *cantus firmus* in G
Two examples on the *cantus firmus* in A
Two examples on the *cantus firmus* in C

At the bottom of the page, again marginal remarks by Albrechtsberger (see p. 66).

**6**

---

*Fourth Species of Two-Part Counterpoint*
Marginal text by Albrechtsberger (see p. 67 f.)
Two examples on the *cantus firmus* in D
Two examples on the *cantus firmus* in E
Two examples on the *cantus firmus* in F
Two examples on the *cantus firmus* in G
Two examples on the *cantus firmus* in A

With the annotations at the bottom of the page, Albrechtsberger's commentary is concluded (see p. 67). Beethoven's original version in the ninth line read apparently

instead of

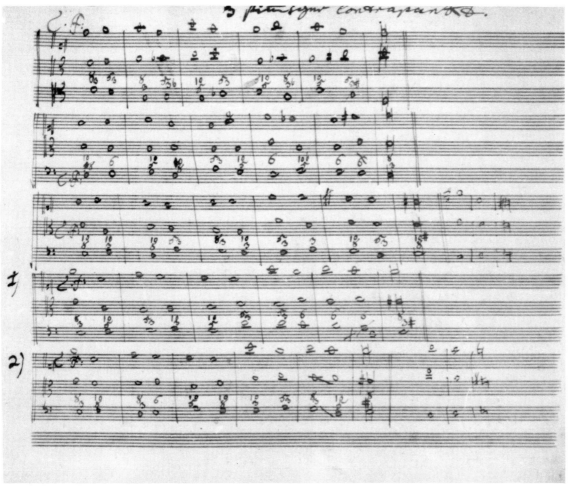

7

---

*THREE-PART COUNTERPOINT*
Two examples, now separately notated, on the *cantus firmus* in D
One example on the *cantus firmus* in E
Two further examples, marked 1) and 2) on the *cantus firmus* in E

Haydn's annotations begin on this page with measures entered in the margin and the change from a to d in the bass part of the fourth exercise. With the exception of the entry at the bottom of the page, they are regularly marked with a cross or a similar symbol. The lines indicating hidden parallels, here and on the following page, were apparently entered by Beethoven. Throughout the first three species of three-part counterpoint, Beethoven added figures (at times crossed to indicate sharping) in order to clarify interval relationships with the lowest part; the third is occasionally represented merely by a sharp.

*8*

A concluding example on the *cantus firmus* in E
Three examples on the *cantus firmus* in F
One example on the *cantus firmus* in G

    The letter h (denoting  b♮ ) is entered for the first note on the page; the letter e is entered for the second note of the top part in the second exercise; and the letter h appears again in the top part of the last exercise (to point out the correction from a).

    The change from c to e in the top part of the first exercise was probably made by Beethoven to avoid hidden fifths, as are others on this page. In the penultimate measure of the third exercise, Beethoven corrected a unison between the top and middle parts. The figures in the third measure of the fourth exercise were obviously entered after the change to the note a had been made (apparently from alternate versions containing b♭ and d).

**9**

Two further examples on the *cantus firmus* in G
Three examples on the *cantus firmus* in A

As the correction in the second example shows, the interval numbers were again entered subsequently, the changes in notes having been made immediately in the process of copying the part.

*10*

Three examples on the *cantus firmus* in C

*Second Species of Three-Part Counterpoint*
Two examples on the *cantus firmus* in D

Haydn corrects a succession of parallel octaves in the second measure of the last example, writing out the part in half notes again at the bottom of the page (and entering the alternate notes a and f for the second beat).

*11*

A further example on the *cantus firmus* in D
Three examples on the *cantus firmus* in E
One example on the *cantus firmus* in F

Beethoven adds "cis" (c♯) to the last note of measure 4 in the first example and enters a choice of high and low d for the end of the bass part. In measure 3 of the second example, the last figure is erroneously given as 4 instead of 2. In measure 3 of the third example, Beethoven entered a choice of b and g for the second half note (the small mark above the notes possibly belonging to a letter g entered to indicate preference for the latter). The second 8 in the following measure apparently refers to the upper voice.

Haydn corrects the cadence in the third example and changes the beginning on a to one on e in the fourth example. The corrected part in half notes reads:

Nottebohm noted parallel fifths between alto and bass in the progression from the first to the second measure of the third example.

**12**

Three further examples on the *cantus firmus* in F, the latter two marked 1) and 2)
Two examples on the *cantus firmus* in G

The figure 3 in the third measure of the first example refers to the middle part; that in measure 4, to the upper part. In the last example, Beethoven crossed the first figure in measure 3 and added a sharp.

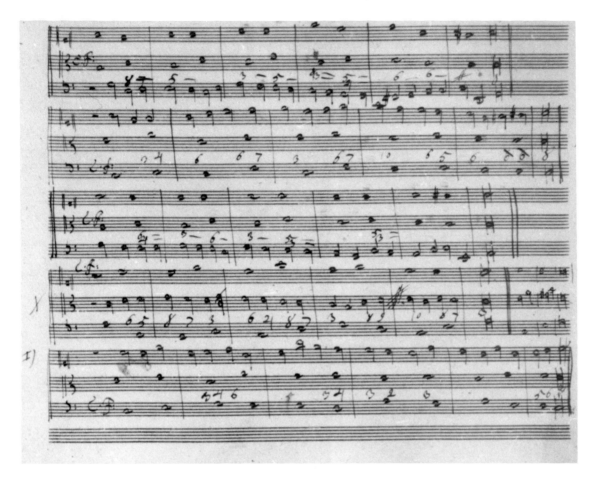

*13*

A further example on the *cantus firmus* in G
Three examples on the *cantus firmus* in A
One example on the *cantus firmus* in C, marked as 1)
of two alternate solutions.

Beethoven makes several errors in entering the figures.

Haydn corrects hidden fifths between measures 2 and 3 and hidden octaves in measure 5 of the fourth example, adding in the latter case the leading tone to the cadence (Nottebohm argues that this should have been placed as the penultimate note of the part).

*14*

Three further examples on the *cantus firmus* in C, the first of which is marked 2) as the alternate example for the last on the preceding page.

Beethoven enters a change in measure 3 of the first example to avoid parallel octaves.

**15**

*Third Species of Three-Part Counterpoint*
Three examples on the *cantus firmus* in D
One example on the *cantus firmus* in E

As the first measure of the second example suggests, Beethoven thinks of b♭ as a norm within the larger melodic context of the Dorian melody. He changes the natural sign back to flat in example 2, measure 2 and example 3, measure 2.

*16*

Two further examples on the *cantus firmus* in E          The alternate version in example 3 is Beethoven's
Two examples on the *cantus firmus* in F                   own.

**17**

A further example on the *cantus firmus* in F
Three examples on the *cantus firmus* in G

Beethoven changes a progression into an open fifth in the first example.

Haydn changes the second and third bass notes in the third example in order to obtain a full chord on the downbeat and to avoid the suggestion of parallel octaves. He changes the first note of the bass part in the fourth measure of the last example again in favor of a full three-part sound on the downbeat. The correction is obviously made in haste, without taking note of the change in the *cantus firmus* or the wrong clef in the middle part (alto instead of tenor). Haydn takes no exception to the open fourth as a chord tone (penultimate quarter in the same measure).

*18*

Three examples on the *cantus firmus* in A
One example on the *cantus firmus* in C

Beethoven changes a to e in the first measure of
the third example to avoid a unison between soprano
and alto parts, and changes c to a in the penultimate
measure.

Haydn corrects the free dissonance on b in the
second measure of the last example, converting the
quarter-note figure into the cambiata pattern. The
second quarter note in the fourth measure, resulting
in an open fourth, is used as a chord tone (cf. the
preceding page).

*19*

---

Two further examples on the *cantus firmus* in C

*Fourth Species of Three-Part Counterpoint*
Two examples on the *cantus firmus* in D

Beethoven enters an alternate version for the fourth measure of the first example and changes the second quarter note d in the last measure to avoid the suggestion of parallel octaves. In the second measure of the last example, the open fourth on c again occurs in a chordal context. Beethoven changes the first note in the upper voice of the next measure to avoid a unison and marks the following note by the letter d.

**20**

A further example on the *cantus firmus* in D
Three examples on the *cantus firmus* in E

Beethoven began the top part of the second example a third too low. Starting with the part in syncopations, his manuscript suggests once again the process of copying from an earlier draft, as does the frequent poor alignment of notes, both vertically and horizontally. In the third measure of example 3, Beethoven apparently changed g to d in order to avoid delayed octaves.

*21*

Three examples on the *cantus firmus* in F
One example on the *cantus firmus* in G

Beethoven marks the first note in the middle part of the first example with the letter c and the last note of the top part in example 4, measure 3, with the letter h (b♮).

Regarding the penultimate measure of example 2, cf. notes for pp. *17* and *18*.

22

Three further examples on the *cantus firmus* in G, the second and third of which are again marked 1) and 2) as alternate solutions.

One example on the *cantus firmus* in A, also marked 1), for which the alternate solution, however, is missing (cf. p. 73).

Beethoven uses the tenor instead of the alto clef for the middle part of example 2. The open fourth preceding the cadence of the third example enters on a pedal point effected by voice crossing.

23

The exercises in the fifth species begin with three examples on the *cantus firmus* in A, followed by two examples on the *cantus firmus* in C (the preceding examples are apparently lost; cf. p. 72).

Beethoven's change in the florid part of the fourth example seems to have been prompted by motivic interest, while in the florid part of the fifth example, he wanted to create a melodic high point. (The change in the upper voice was apparently made in order to avoid the direct motion into the fifth between alto and soprano parts in the next measure.)

*24*

---

The last example on the *cantus firmus* in C for the fifth species of three-part counterpoint

The seventh arising in the second half of the first measure is one of several free dissonances not noted by Nottebohm. The change in the fourth measure was apparently made to avoid the resolution into a unison.

*FOUR-PART COUNTERPOINT*

Three examples on the *cantus firmus* in D

The first four-part exercise contains a cadential $^6_4$ chord (the fourth is used as a prepared dissonance; cf. the third example on page *22*).

The clef for the second part of the last exercise was changed from alto to tenor.

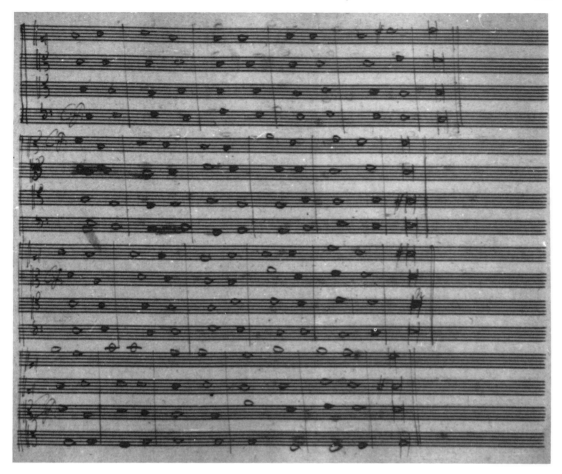

25

---

A further example on the *cantus firmus* in D
Three examples on the *cantus firmus* in E

The changes in the first two measures of example 2 apparently resulted from the correction of the alto into a tenor clef. (Similar problems appear repeatedly due to the use of the same clef for different voices.)

*26*

A further example on the *cantus firmus* in E
Three examples on the *cantus firmus* in F

The notes in the second bass measure of the first example are clarified by the letters d and c, and Beethoven places the letter c again in the first and third measures of the last exercise, as he corrects various errors in the bass part.

27

Two examples, representing alternate solutions, on the *cantus firmus* in F
Three examples on the *cantus firmus* in G

Beethoven places two examples next to each other in the first four-part system, entering the word "oder" (or) above the second. Haydn's corrections for the examples in the second and fourth systems (those for the latter made in pencil) are concerned with the cross relation f - f♯; his corrections of the example in the third system, with the direct motion into a unison. As on page *17*, he takes no note of a wrong clef (alto instead of tenor in the third part of the second system) or of the change in the *cantus firmus* (third system).

28

Another example on the *cantus firmus* in G
Three examples on the *cantus firmus* in A

The "NB" placed next to the third system apparently points out another case of close registers, resulting in unisons and voice-crossing.

29

---

A further example on the *cantus firmus* in A
Three examples on the *cantus firmus* in C

Haydn changes f to a in the third measure of the second example to avoid direct motion into a fifth. His correction raises the interesting question of why he dealt with this particular case and not with numerous similar ones in these pages. The reason may be that in this instance, the progression constitutes what

Fux refers to as a "quinta battuta"—a fifth that is emphasized by a step (here the *mi-fa* half tone) in the low part and a skip in the high part.

Beethoven changes the first note in the second part, example 4, measure 4, from a (which would have formed a unison, reached by direct motion, with the part below) to f and marks two other changes in the measure by the letters d and a.

*30*

The last example on the *cantus firmus* in C for the first species of four-part counterpoint
Beginning of Four-Part Counterpoint in the Second Species
Two examples on the *cantus firmus* in D

The final note c in the second part of the first example is changed to e (by Haydn?). Haydn corrects parallel fifths in the fourth measure of the second example by placing e as the second half note in the soprano part. It is not clear whether the second half note c in the second measure comes also from Haydn's pen. While it serves as a correction for the unresolved dissonance caused by b♭, the change is made without regard for the context: the progression from c to the following half note a would cause parallel fifths. (There are other cases of spot corrections that may not have been meant to be considered in context.) The changes in the tenor and bass parts, measures 3–4, are Beethoven's own.

*31*

Two examples on the *cantus firmus* in D
Two examples on the *cantus firmus* in E

Beethoven marks the first tenor note of measure 3 in the second example with the letter c.

Haydn changes the last two notes of the tenor part in the second example; this modification converts the penultimate chord, containing the tone e in three parts, into a full triad. Nottebohm notes that it also removes the direct motion into a fifth (tenor and bass parts) but that it introduces a free seventh into the alto part of the penultimate measure. Haydn corrects parallel fifths between the two lower parts in the progression from the first to the second measure of example 3 (also a succession of three octaves, evidently a copying error, between the second and bottom parts).

The sharp in the top part at the end of the last example is apparently valid.

*32*

Two examples on the *cantus firmus* in E
Two examples on the *cantus firmus* in F

The second note in the second part of the first example, measure 4, is marked with the letter h (b ♮).  The
first note of the penultimate measure in the tenor part
of the second example is changed to b.

33

---

Two examples on the *cantus firmus* in F
Two examples on the *cantus firmus* in G

The third measure of the bass part of the first example
is changed from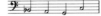

to

Beethoven rewrites measures 2 to 5 of the original
version for the second example (which contains parallel fifths between the alto and bass parts in the
fourth measure), placing the word "oder" (or) above
the alternate version.

The first half note in the third example, measure 3. is
changed and marked h (b♮); the first note in the
preceding measure of the alto part is marked e.

Beethoven copied from the third instead of the second
measure after the opening measure of the last example, then tried to correct the mistake but eventually
crossed out the whole example in order to recopy it
on the next page (see p. 65).

34

Three examples on the *cantus firmus* in G
One example on the *cantus firmus* in A

Haydn corrects the cross relation f-f♯ occurring between the third and fourth measures of the first example, at the same time removing a free dissonance arising between the two upper parts in measure 4.

Beethoven changes the fourth measure of the top part in example 2 in order to avoid parallel octaves with the bass.

Haydn corrects parallel fifths in the third and fourth measures of the third example, rewriting the passage at the margin.

35

Three examples on the *cantus firmus* in A
One example on the *cantus firmus* in C

Beethoven changes the first note of the bass part in the fourth measure of the last example in order to avoid direct motion into a fifth between the outer parts (the correction results in direct motion into an octave between an outer and an inner part, which is more regularly tolerated in the examples).

*36*

Three further examples on the *cantus firmus* in C

Beginning of Four-Part Counterpoint in the Third Species
One example on the *cantus firmus* in D

Beethoven changes the beginning of the first example in order to avoid parallel octaves and gives two alternate solutions (high and low g instead of c). He changes the second note of the tenor part in the penultimate measure to c (probably from e, in order to avoid octaves with the top part).

In the second example, Beethoven changes the first note of the second part in measure 2 to b (marked by the letter h) and the second note of the top part in the same measure to c. Haydn changes the first note in measure 4 of the second part in the same example to a (avoiding direct motion into an octave with the top part) As Nottebohm notes, parallel octaves between the second and bottom parts in the penultimate measure remained uncorrected.

The last example on the page contains Beethoven's entries of the letters c, d, and a to clarify the respective notes. The second measure of the top part is understood to include b♭ (cf. the comment for page *15*, second example).

37

---

Three examples on the *cantus firmus* in D
One example on the *cantus firmus* in E

The last quarter note of the second measure in the first example is corrected to read b♭; the last quarter note of the following measure is corrected to read b♮. Parallel fifths between the soprano and tenor parts in measures 3–4 remained uncorrected.
Beethoven wrote e and a for the first note of the alto part in measure 4 of the second example but rejected the latter (which would be reached by direct motion into an octave and result in a unison with the soprano part), confirming the choice of e by the added letter.

In example 3, Beethoven eliminated a rest for the beginning of the bass part; a succession of octaves between alto and bass in the third measure were left uncorrected. The use of the turning note g in the penultimate measure corresponds to accepted classical practice (it is similarly applied in Thomas Attwood's studies with Mozart and also in Fux's text).

Beethoven corrects the second bass note in the second measure of the last example to read e (adding the letter) and the last quarter note of the measure to read d.

38

Three further examples on the *cantus firmus* in E
One example on the *cantus firmus* in F

Haydn's corrections in this segment of Beethoven's
work offer characteristic suggestions for the improvement of the extended melodic line, of which his
change in the penultimate measure of the first exercise
is a primary example. He converted a grouping of
two-note fragments into a melodic entity that, through
the addition of the tone e, avoids the threefold use of
d for the highest tone as well as the emphasis on the
diminished fifth (see p. 69).

Beethoven entered several corrections in the quarter
note melody of the second exercise; a succession of
octaves between tenor and bass parts in the penultimate measure was left uncorrected.

Haydn places the note f (in pencil) at the beginning
of the quarter note melody for the last example in
order to confirm the beginning in the mode of F.
Beethoven changes the second tenor note in the fourth
measure in order to avoid direct motion into an octave
and parallel octaves in the progression to the next
measure.

*39*

Three further examples on the *cantus firmus* in F
One example on the *cantus firmus* in G

In the second measure of the first example, Haydn corrects the tenor note d to read c in order to avoid parallel fifths.

Beethoven changes the second quarter note in the third measure of the second example to avoid the suggestion of parallel fifths with the bass part.

Haydn improves the sonority of the first chord in the third example. The change of the second note in the third measure of the soprano part from f to g is apparently Beethoven's own.

Nottebohm notes the unprepared seventh (with the tenor part) arising through the third quarter note in the second measure of the last example.

Haydn corrects a succession of octaves in the penultimate and final measures of the last example, placing the last two tenor notes an octave lower; accordingly, he also introduces the leading tone of the bass part an octave lower and indicates with the annotation "8^va bassa" that the entire succession of the last five notes in the bass part should be transposed. His entries on this page were all made in pencil.

*40*

---

Three further examples on the *cantus firmus* in G

One example on the *cantus firmus* in A

Haydn's change in the opening measure of the first example is concerned with the correction of parallel fifths between the alto and bass parts, but in altering the downward sequence of step and skip (the skip occurring from a diminished fifth formed with the tenor part), he also converts the passage into a more highly integrated melody. In accordance with the corrected version, f is changed to f♯ in the opening measures of the next two examples.

Haydn corrects parallel unisons in measures 1 and 2 of the last example, placing the first bass note an octave lower. The other corrections in the example are Beethoven's own. He clarifies the change to e in the fourth measure of the tenor part again by writing in the letter; the change in the penultimate bass measure was made to avoid a succession of fifths with the soprano part.

41

Three further examples on the *cantus firmus* in A
One example on the *cantus firmus* in C

Beethoven marks the second bass note in the first example with the letter a. Haydn, again in pencil, corrects the last quarter note of the third measure to avoid hidden fifths with the soprano (cf. Nottebohm's comment mentioned on p. 70). The fifths between measures 4 and 5 in the alto and tenor parts were pointed out by Nottebohm. Concerning the open fourth resulting in the second half of measure 4 in the bass part of the third example, cf. page *17*, last example. Concerning the turning note in the penultimate measure, cf. page *37*, third example.

*42*

Two further examples on the *cantus firmus* in C

Beginning of Four-Part Counterpoint in the Fourth Species

Two examples on the *cantus firmus* in D

The corrected tenor part for the fifth measure of the first example reads:

A succession of fifths (from a diminished into a perfect fifth) between the soprano and tenor parts of the preceding measure was left unchanged. Beethoven replaced a with c in the tenor part of the first measure in the second example. Concerning measures 4 and 6 of the bass part, again cf. pages *17* and *37*, respectively.

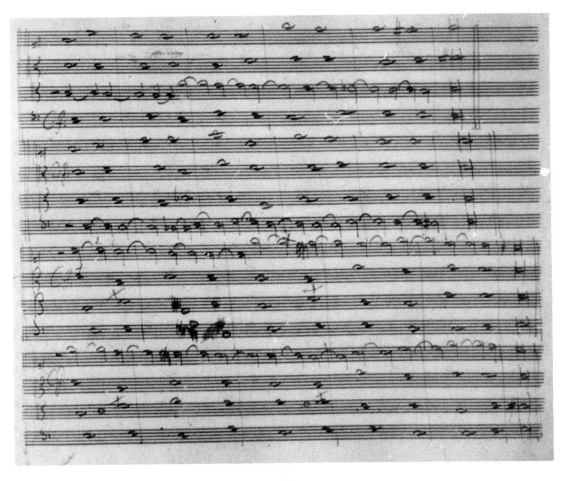

*43*

Two examples on the *cantus firmus* in D
Two examples on the *cantus firmus* in E, marked 1) and 2)

Haydn, whose annotations continue to appear in pencil throughout the exercises in this species, marks crosses for the last two notes of the soprano part in measure 1 of the third example as well as for the first note in the alto part and the second note in the tenor part. The voice crossing in the latter two parts suggests delayed fifths with the soprano whose resolution to the note a is at the same time anticipated in the alto. In the third measure of the example, Haydn enters crosses again to mark another anticipation of the tone of resolution. The other changes in this

example, as well as the change in the second measure of the last example, are Beethoven's own.

The opening of the second example shows the accepted use of the open fourth in a chordal context.

In the first measure of the last example, Haydn changes the tenor note d (also marked by a cross) to a in order to avoid a further anticipation of the dissonance resolution. Haydn's correction in the third measure of the example shows that, while he accepts the doubling of the resolution tone in this case, he is concerned with avoiding the resolution into a sixth chord, though not all such instances are marked. (Fux's solution to this problem is to place two different half notes in one of the parts consisting otherwise of whole notes.)

44

---

Three further examples on the *cantus firmus* in E., the first two marked as alternate solutions 1) and 2) One example on the *cantus firmus* in F

Haydn's comment on the first and second examples deals essentially with the same problem as that in the third measure of the last example on the preceding page, but it now becomes apparent that his criticism is directed in particular at the 4–3 resolution into the sixth chord; he marks the recurring sixth chords in the second example with crosses and the figure 6. (His corrections in the first example involve a change in the *cantus firmus*). The change from e to a for the second tenor note in measure 2 of the first example is apparently Beethoven's own.

In accordance with eighteenth-century practice, Beethoven uses the progression of a diminished fifth in the cadential formula (soprano part, example 3).

*45*

Three further examples on the *cantus firmus* in F
One example on the *cantus firmus* in G

Haydn, marking five large crosses at the left margin to indicate his various corrections, points out the 4–3 resolution into the sixth chord again in the opening measure of the first example and rewrites its beginning at the right margin. In measure 3, he marks only the anticipation of the resolution tone. Beethoven changed the second tenor note in measure 2 to avoid hidden fifths with the top part.

In the second example, Haydn changes the first soprano note of the second measure from f to a and marks the anticipated resolution of the interval of the fourth by adding the figures 3 and 4.

In the third example, Haydn notes delayed fifths (entering the figure 5 twice, as well as crosses, to point out the juxtaposition of triads on d and c). Beethoven changed the second alto note in measure 2 from c to a.

In the last example, Haydn changes the first tenor note of the second measure from g (the anticipated resolution tone, marked with a cross) to e.

46

Three examples on the *cantus firmus* in G

One example on the *cantus firmus* in A

Beethoven changes the second soprano note in example 1, measure 2, to avoid a dissonance with the last half note in the alto part, and he changes the first soprano note in example 2, measure 3, to correct parallel fifths with the bass.

Haydn changes the first note, measure 2, in the second part of example 3 from d to b in correcting the delayed fifths he had marked in the second and bottom parts. Beethoven marks the second note in the third part, measure 4, with the letter e; the second note in the second part, measure 5, with the letter g; and the first note in the bass part, example 4, measure 4, with the letter h (b♮).

The third example is begun on a sixth chord. The downbeat of example 3, measure 4, is formed by a fourth, used, as in earlier instances, in a chordal context.

*47*

Three further examples on the *cantus firmus* in A
One example on the *cantus firmus* in C

Of the various instances in which Haydn evidently condones anticipating the tone of resolution, the penutimate measure of the second example is the most interesting, for it also involves the 4–3 resolution into the sixth chord that he normally forbids; the latter, however, including the leading tone, assumes a cadential function in this case. The tenor clef in the third part of example 3 was changed to the alto clef.

*48*

Four additional examples on the *cantus firmus* in C

Beethoven changed the first note in the alto part of example 1, measure 4, from f to a. He corrected a to c in the bass part of example 3, measure 3, to avoid parallel octaves with the soprano part but evidently overlooked parallel octaves between the soprano and tenor parts in the cadence of the last example.

*The last six pages of the manuscript were wrongly placed and paginated after the manuscript passed out of Beethoven's hands (the pagination throughout is not Beethoven's own). They are here presented in what must have been the original order, following the sequence of modes on D, E, F, G, A, and C: pages 51, 52, 53, 54, 49, 50.*

*51*

---

Four examples on the *cantus firmus* in D

This final portion of Beethoven's manuscript, which is marred by ink spots, exhibits its most regular layout—four exercises each on six pages covering the six modes, respectively—but it appears to have been more hastily compiled than the preceding sections. This is evident in various details: bar lines are at times wrongly placed, alternate solutions for the same distribution of *cantus firmus* and free voices are no longer so marked, and the melodic design tends to be more perfunctory than in the corresponding three-part examples. Haydn's review continues, but it, too, suggests comparatively greater haste; unlike those in the third and fourth species of four-part counterpoint, his subsequent corrections are not concerned with new problems of part-writing, and they appear less frequently.

Nottebohm suggests that Haydn's correction, changing the soprano part in the first measure of the first example from  to

was made in order to convert the opening chord into a complete triad; at the same time, it strengthens the melodic contour. Beethoven changes the sixth note in the bass part of the same example from d to f to avoid parallel fifths with the tenor part in the progression to the following measure. Regarding the cadence of the third example, cf. the comment for page *47*.

The end of the first measure in the bass part of the last example, originally containing an unresolved dissonance formed by the last note g, was crossed out, but the corrected version of the measure is not clear. The penultimate measure of the same part contains the quarter note pattern involving a turning dissonance (cf. p. 37) which recurs in the exercises on the next three *cantus firmi*. Beethoven changed the last soprano note of the example from a to f.

52

---

Four examples on the *cantus firmus* in E

Haydn corrects the first measure of the first example and the fourth measure of the second example in order to avoid the 4–3 resolution into the sixth chord. He changes the first alto note in the penultimate measure of the second example to obtain a full chord. Regarding the progression of a seventh arising from two successive corrections in the tenor part, cf. p. *30*.

In his unusual formation of the cadence for the third example, Beethoven disregarded the irregular resolution of the agumented fourth formed by the last quarter note in the florid part. He changed the second measure in the soprano part of the last example in order to avoid parallel octaves with the *cantus firmus*, continued to alter the melodic line in the following measure (avoiding the anticipation of the resolution tone f), and marked the first soprano note in the fourth measure with the letter d.

53

Four examples on the *cantus firmus* in F

The parallel fifths occurring in the progression from the third to the fourth measure of the second example between the alto and bass parts remained uncorrected.

Haydn marks the unison between soprano and alto parts in the 4–3 resolution to a sixth chord occurring in the first measure of the third example.

*54*

Four examples on the *cantus firmus* in G

Held against the light, portions of the page that are blotted out by the ink spot remain barely legible, especially in the top line. With the alto part provided by the *cantus firmus*, the transition from measures 3 and 4 to measure 5 of the first example may be reconstructed as follows:

A reconstruction of the second and third examples is rendered less difficult since almost all the passages blotted out involve the *cantus firmus:*

In the bottom part of the first example, the tenor clef was changed to a bass clef.

Haydn marked parallel fifths occurring between the soprano and bass parts in the progression from measure 2 to measure 3 of the second example and corrected the passage by changing the second soprano note in measure 2 to g and the second tenor note to b.

Using the opening melodic formula from the second and third examples in the florid part of the last example, Beethoven began with a sixth chord and overlooked the preceding open fourth. The second and third measures of the bottom part read:

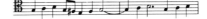

*49*

---

Four examples on the *cantus firmus* in A

The soprano part of the first example begins with a half rest followed by a dotted half note e. What Beethoven crossed out in the fourth measure of the same part was apparently a quarter note g followed by two eighth notes, a and b.

In his correction for the second measure in the tenor part of the third example, Beethoven marked the first of the newly entered notes with the letter f. Regarding the cadence of the same example, cf. the comment for page *47*.

*50*

Four examples on the *cantus firmus* in C

The reading of the fifth measure in the soprano part of the first example, is obscured by the erroneously placed bar line. The first alto note in the same measure is marked with the letter g.

The soprano note f in the final measure of the second example was apparently added as an after-thought, but the progression f-e must have been considered the valid one because the parallel progression in the tenor part was changed to f-g.

# Schubert's Lesson with Sechter
# Fugal Answer

---

*Schubert's Lesson with Sechter*

143

2.

3.

3.

4.

4.

5.                                        5.

5.

6.

6.

7.

7.

8.

8.

*Sechter's Explanations*

ins
E mol

(see p. 148)

Sechter's Fugue
Dedicated to Schubert's memory

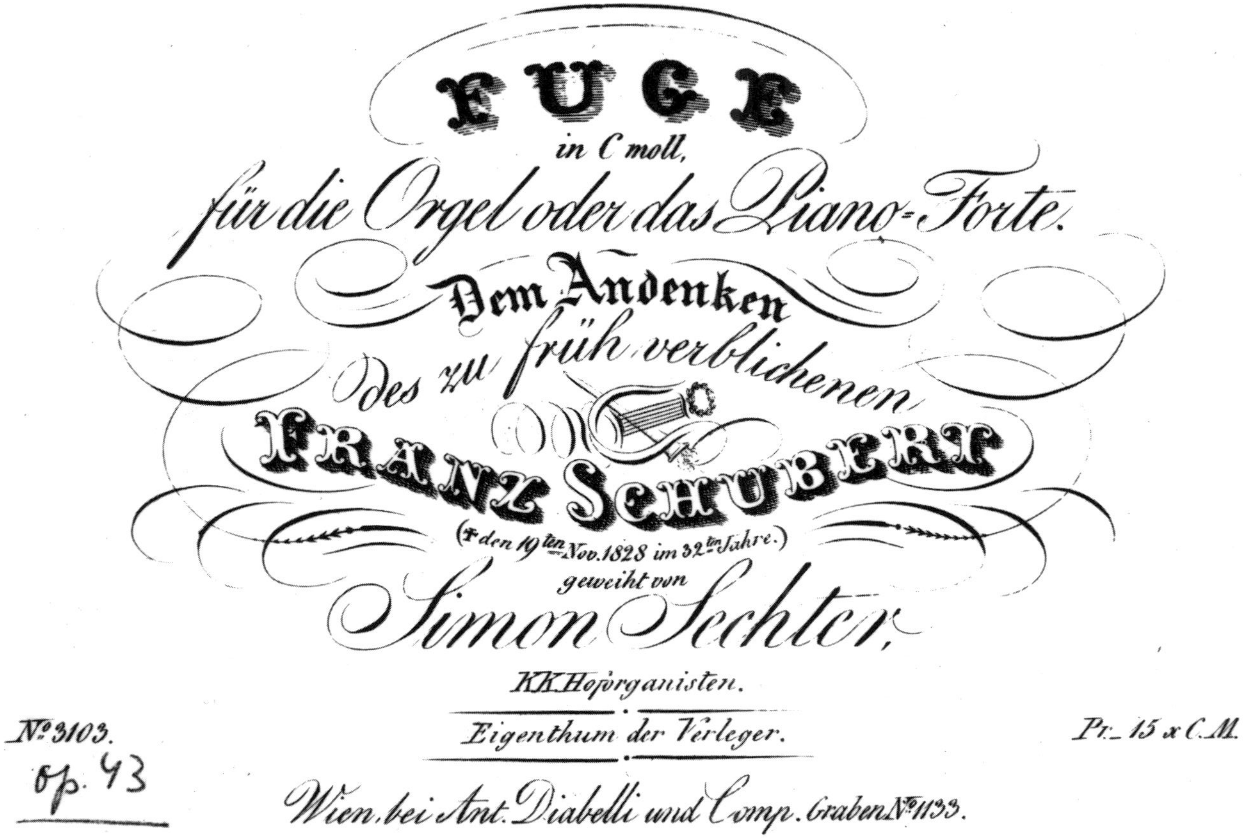

FUGE
in C moll,
für die Orgel oder das Piano-Forte.
Dem Andenken
des zu früh verblichenen
FRANZ SCHUBERT
(✝ den 19ten Nov. 1828 im 32ten Jahre.)
geweiht von
Simon Sechter,
K.K. Hoforganisten.
№ 3103.
op. 43
Eigenthum der Verleger.
Pr. 15 x C.M.
Wien, bei Ant. Diabelli und Comp. Graben № 1133.

# ·V·

## The Decline of
## Conventional Theory

SCHUBERT's historic lesson with Sechter represents theory's "finest hour," and the immin-
ence of a decline can be sensed in reviewing the steps in the composer's pursuit of formal
studies from Salieri to Sechter.

Salieri's tutelage stressed the art of *bel canto,* and there is no question that Schubert's
vocal writing benefited from the experience. But it was the technique of instrumental,
rather than vocal, composition that interested Schubert at that time, and the questions of
structure, thematic development, and harmonic design that had occupied him were, to his
mind, embodied in the exploration of fugal counterpoint.

Italian didactic tradition had moved away from fugal technique. We know what Fux
thought of the fugal art of Italian *professori,* and a telling comment is contained in the set of
Italian studies that Attwood took to Mozart. Here, the matter of fugal answer had still
been explained in terms of Zarlino's two basic divisions of the octave: "arithmetic" (fourth
and fifth) and "harmonic" (fifth and fourth). To these two divisions Attwood had added in
his notes the "mathematic" and "geometric" divisions, but they had no meaning for him,
and the latter he designated, by mistake, as the "geographic division."

In seeking clarification of the principles of writing counterpoint, Schubert had moved
not only from Italian to German teaching traditions but also from the composer's workshop
to the studio of the theorist. The principles of technique that formed the substance of his
lesson with Sechter were based on past, not present styles. The critical questions that had
begun to arise by this time in the nineteenth century were: which of these principles were
still valid?—which required modification?

At the threshold of a new age in the pedagogy of composition stands, Janus-like, the
mysterious figure of another Italian composer who, like Salieri, had assumed a dominant
didactic role north of the Alps: Luigi Cherubini. This Florentine master was a genuine
disciple of Italian schooling as he had been trained by Guiseppe Sarti, one of the foremost
students of Padre Martini. But having settled in Paris early in his career, he embraced the
imposing and complex dramatic style characteristic of the French Revolution. While he
never abandoned the legacy of the old contrapuntal art, it remained merely enshrined in

his later works. His eminent calling was that of a teacher, but in a totally novel way: he became one of the five *Inspecteurs* of the newly-founded Paris Conservatory and subsequently its director. Though he lived in constant conflict with Napoleon, his rule as a modern musical administrator was truly Napoleonic; yet it also reflected the age of Revolution, for his teaching was aimed at class instruction on a large scale.

The most famous of the early theory textbooks was his *Cours de contrepoint et de fugue* (1837), but like his creative work, his theoretical writing contains ambiguities. This may be due, in part at least, to the fact that he insisted on drafting the text in French, which he never fully mastered. The book was actually published by his student Jacques Fromental Halévy, and its formulation suggests the typical estrangement between author and reader which was to persist throughout the era of textbook instruction.

Documentation of the work of teacher and student, face to face, now becomes a rarity. An addendum to the recently edited correspondence of Berlioz contains a letter from the composer to Humbert Ferrand, a young friend, which provides a record, however isolated and brief, of the emergence of new issues and standards:

10 March 1862

My dear Humbert,

I am returning your Lament, without having added an accompaniment, in order to tell you that your modulation from A [major] to B [minor] makes it nearly unperformable. Not that the transition from A to B is poorly carried out, but because it is impossible to begin again in A at the second strophe without unbearable harshness. Besides, a lament should not involve such ambitious modulations. Certainly one can make songs beginning in one key and ending in another on the condition that the two keys are closely related. Thus I began the Peasants' Dance in *[The Damnation of] Faust* in E minor and ended it in G. But the return to E after the G chord is very pleasing and very easy. I have marked the change I propose making in your melody; you should stay in A from beginning to end, only modulating to A minor for the five measures before the fermata. The return to A major will produce without harshness the effect you were seeking in modulating to B.

If you accept what I have said, I will do the accompaniment for you. And even if you don't. But I assure you the girls and boys in the countryside won't sing your song, and the amateurs, helped by the piano accompaniment, will make faces when they begin the second and subsequent strophes, and the musicians will say, "Someone made a mistake in copying the song" . . .[1]

In Mendelssohn's lessons with Karl Friedrich Zelter one still perceives the authority of Bach: Zelter had studied with Kirnberger. But Wagner, who studied with Christian Theodor Weinlig, one of Bach's successors at St. Thomas's, found himself subjected to a different type of authority. In his *Manual of Fugue* (1845), Weinlig gave preference to his own examples as study models over the work of his great predecessor, because they contained "nothing that might confuse or divert the student." The teaching of fugue eventually degenerated into the "examination fugue," the antithesis of Bach's fugal writing:

---

[1] Ralph P. Locke, "New Letters of Berlioz," *19th Century Music*, I (1977), no. 1.

. . . the student would be ill-advised to take the first fugue of the Forty-Eight as a model for examination work . . . Neither is the second fugue of the Forty-Eight a good model for examination . . .[2]

The changing attitude toward traditional principles appears most clearly in the weakening of the cardinal rule against parallel fifths and octaves. The situation is elucidated in the highly interesting correspondence of Tchaikovsky with Vladislav Albertovich Pakhulsky, a young composer who had submitted compositions to him for review.

In Tchaikovsky's letters, the composer speaks to the composer, and Tchaikovsky touches on details dealing with form, orchestration, and prosody. But he feels himself compelled to speak also as a "theorist," and in doing so, his advice becomes apologetic, though it remains firm:

Well then, a teacher of harmony is forever within me, and I can't help but persecute *octaves* and *fifths* . . . by an old habit, I could not refrain from fussing at your writing octaves in the outer voices. Please correct this![3]

Nevertheless, he modifies his stand as soon as it is taken:

Perhaps this is just an eccentricity of mine, but I have a certain right to it because I positively avoid fifths and octaves myself, except for cases where it is obvious to everyone that they are used intentionally for the sake of a characteristic effect.

Similarly, Tchaikovsky remarks in connection with a passage he had criticized:

Such octave passages can be good if they appear for a special reason in a whole series of chords, but here . . . they shook me terribly.

In another letter, he reiterates

. . . please check the part writing once more, so that nobody like me could cavil at anything.

He does not allude to the new complexities of part writing resulting from the enrichment of orchestration, but he changes one instance of parallels by adding more of them, saying "When the whole orchestra is playing, the middle must be full" (Example V–1). Conversely, he marks parallel octaves in two of the scores submitted to him later, though he adds: "But I will stop pestering you with my mania to root out *fifths* and *octaves* everywhere" (Examples V–2 and V–3).

Tchaikovsky's most severe criticism is directed, however, at pieces written as exercises, and it is evident that his role as an adviser of the young colleague does not come into

---

[2] Charles Herbert Kitson, *Studies in Fugue* (London, 1922), p. 48.
[3] This and subsequent quotations of Tchaikovsky can be found in Alfred Mann, "Tchaikovsky as a Teacher," *Music and Civilization*, pp. 279–96. See Foreword, footnote 2.

*Example V–1*

You have it so:                    and it should be so:

*Example V–2*                                                    *Example V–3*

its own until the discussion moved from studies to compositions. In fact, he himself draws the distinction between the advice of teacher and composer: he asks whether the young man's basic instruction was at fault for guiding him without sufficient strictness, and he finally dismisses the matters of basic technique altogether.

That the troublesome question of parallels was uppermost in the mind of the nineteenth-century composer in his role as conscientious craftsman is shown not only in the letters of Tchaikovsky but also in a remarkable document from the hand of Brahms. Entitled *Octaven u. Quinten u. A.* (Octaves, Fifths, and Other Matters), it contains about 140 examples of "faulty" progressions in the works of composers ranging from Palestrina to Bizet, to which Brahms has added his remarks ("very unpleasant to me," "not praiseworthy," "explained or justified easily enough," "intentional fifths," or even "NB beautiful fifths"). To the modern reader the manuscript is available in a particularly interesting form since it was issued in a facsimile edition by Heinrich Schenker who added his own commentary.[4] But his sensitive interpretation singles out a critical point: Brahms is not speaking to a student, and his marginalia represent merely a challenge, not a systematic reformulation, of tutorial rules; they form, as Schenker says, an "artistic soliloquy."

The basic issue of consonance and dissonance proved even more urgent than the problem of parallel fifths and octaves. It is here that theory was particularly helpless in the face of advancing practice, and the breakdown of didactic authority is once more recognizable in the eloquent, increasingly intense testimony of Tchaikovsky's correspondence:

[4] Universal Edition (Vienna, 1933). English translation by Paul Mast in "Brahms's Study, Octaven u. Quinten u. A." in *The Music Forum*, V, (New York, 1980).

I came upon *eleven dissonances in a row*, followed by one accidentally consonant chord, and then four more dissonances—in all, a sequence of sixteen configurations of sound with only one chord to rest the ear!!!!

Listing the basic consonances, he reviews their interaction with dissonances and attempts to reformulate the technique of counterpoint:

All these dissonances give to contrapuntal texture an inexpressible beauty and life, but only on the condition that they are naturally resolved into consonance. It was long before any other combinations of musical sound were tolerated. Eventually citizenship was given to the chord of the dominant seventh, and it grew so independent that its intervals were given the significance of consonances.

One dissonant configuration he had spotted is therefore singled out for his praise (Example V–4), and he goes on to say:

When counterpoint crossed over from the realm of vocal music, little by little, chromaticism and total freedom of modulation penetrated harmony. Beyond this, counterpoint cannot, and must not, go.

*Example V–4*

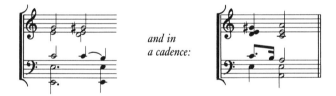

*and in
a cadence:*

He speaks of the "inner ear" that constantly demands that the listener "stop to seek what *shadow* of chord brought together such voices seemingly alien to each other—and at times even the stop does not help." And he admits that contemporary practice has defied the system he is trying to save:

Nevertheless, in our times we occasionally encounter contrapuntal works in which the basic law of counterpoint is completely ignored. You can find dissonances in them in abundance, unprepared, unresolved, and even enjoying such honor and significance as if the whole thing were based on them—as if natural consonant combinations were an unavoidable evil which the composer would willingly skirt if possible.

It happened that I was present at an occasion when a young composer presented a work to Richard Strauss for comment.[5] The piece was a brief composition for piano, and

---

[5] Cf. "The Artistic Testament of Richard Strauss," *The Musical Quarterly*, XXXVI (1950), no. 1.

Strauss, who gave it a careful reading, took exception to the extensive use of dissonance. He added that this might seem a strange criticism coming from the one who had written the *Salome* score. But he explained his argument: what was under discussion was not a score in which greatly differentiated sonorities absorbed what the homogeneous sound of the single medium would only stress. The rise of the symphonic idiom, he pointed out, had placed the use of dissonance in a different light, and he quoted the simultaneous use of suspension and resolution (which had been a subject of Haydn's corrections in Beethoven's exercises) with a "Mozartean" example in which this particular instance of dissonance is justified by the variety of sound inherent in the instrumentation (Example V–5).

*Example V–5*

Strauss was at that time teaching his fourteen-year-old grandson from the pages of Fux's *Gradus ad Parnassum*, the original text of which had practically disappeared since the days of Haydn and Mozart. The twentieth century had placed at the disposal of the composer a range of different sources that was unprecedented, and their availability brought about an essential change in didactic orientation. The maxim of nineteenth-century textbook literature—strict codification—gave way to new insight; the art of part writing was subjected to fresh exploration.

Manuscript notes indicate that Ernest Bloch took with him a volume of the collected works of Lassus on an ocean voyage. "In his forty-eighth year," wrote the daughter of the composer, "he decided that he did not know counterpoint well enough."[6] Using models from the works of Renaissance composers, Bloch wrote out more than twelve hundred studies in strict counterpoint, composing, first of all, his own *cantus firmi* and reviewing them repeatedly in the light of criteria gained in the process. ("This is almost as bad as Bellermann," he remarked about one of them.)

Zoltan Kodály introduced his students to counterpoint by refusing to accept their chorale harmonizations unless the inner parts were enlivened imaginatively; only then were they initiated into formal studies. He gave them excerpts from scores of Haydn quartets from which the viola part had been removed. They were then asked to supply their own versions and compare what they had written with the original. He also gave them copies of Marenzio madrigals without any original or editorial accidentals, leaving to them all decisions regarding cadences and melodic phrase structure.

The spirit of renewed search had begun to influence the exchange of teacher and student. A certain parallel to Tchaikovsky's situation is revealed, but with new conse-

[6]"Ernest Bloch—Student of Choral Music," *American Choral Review*, X (1968), no. 2.

quences, in the pedagogical career of Paul Hindemith. Realizing that he could not presuppose a knowledge of elementary technique in the writing of his students, he interrupted his work on the *Craft of Musical Composition* (1937–1939), a presentation of a modern system of part-writing, to write *A Concentrated Course in Traditional Harmony*, followed by two similar manuals. They were to serve merely as a preparation for advanced training, and in such training the instruction returned to a discussion between composers. Inquiry supplanted rules, and in this, teacher and student were engaged equally. The authority of norms and standards expanded in two directions; the quest for guidance had opened up the road to the models of both past and present.

In the preface to his *Harmonielehre* (1911), Arnold Schoenberg acknowledged his debt to Alban Berg and Anton von Webern, and his text begins with the sentence "This book contains what I have learned from my students." It is relevant to the issue of theory and practice that the figure who exerted the greatest influence upon creative musical thought of the twentieth century stood, as a teacher, so closely aligned with students who shared his level of eminence. Nowhere else in the periods of didactic history discussed in this book was there a similar situation, for even the master-disciple relationship of Haydn and Beethoven remains loose by comparison. Schoenberg's early textbook formulated a theoretical discipline imparted by the composer, and in time the composer formulated a new theory that became living practice. The conflict of the past was resolved; the future was endowed with fresh challenge.

# Index

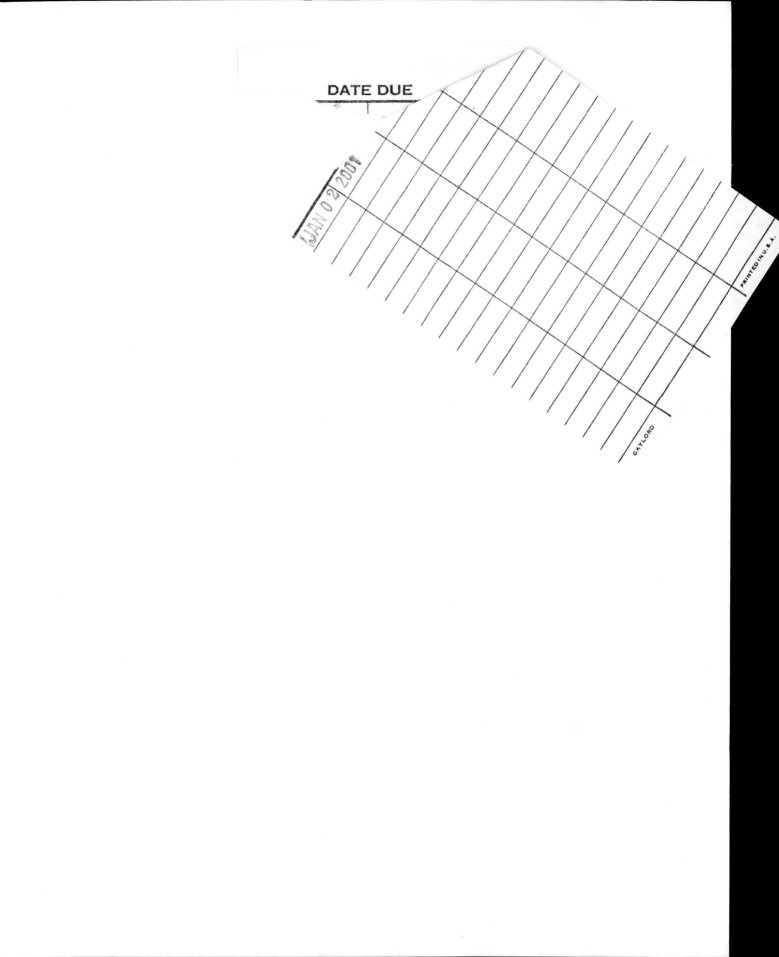

DATE DUE

JAN 0 2 2001